# TEACHER'S PET PUBLICATIONS

## LITPLAN TEACHER PACK
for
The Old Man and the Sea

based on the book by
Ernest Hemingway

Written by
Mary B. Collins

© 1996 Teacher's Pet Publications
All Rights Reserved

This **LitPlan** for Ernest Hemingway's
*The Old Man and The Sea*
has been brought to you by Teacher's Pet Publications, Inc.

Copyright Teacher's Pet Publications 1996
11504 Hammock Point
Berlin MD 21811

Only the student materials in this unit plan
such as worksheets, study questions, assignment sheets, and tests
may be reproduced multiple times for use in the purchaser's classroom.

For any additional copyright questions,
contact Teacher's Pet Publications.

www.tpet.com

TABLE OF CONTENTS - *The Old Man and the Sea*

| | |
|---|---|
| Introduction | 5 |
| Unit Objectives | 8 |
| Reading Assignment Sheet | 9 |
| Unit Outline | 10 |
| Study Questions (Short Answer) | 13 |
| Quiz/Study Questions (Multiple Choice) | 20 |
| Pre-reading Vocabulary Worksheets | 35 |
| Lesson One (Introductory Lesson) | 45 |
| Nonfiction Assignment Sheet | 60 |
| Oral Reading Evaluation Form | 48 |
| Writing Assignment 1 | 58 |
| Writing Assignment 2 | 62 |
| Writing Assignment 3 | 68 |
| Writing Evaluation Form | 63 |
| Vocabulary Review Activities | 56 |
| Extra Writing Assignments/Discussion ?s | 54 |
| Unit Review Activities | 65 |
| Unit Tests | 71 |
| Unit Resource Materials | 97 |
| Vocabulary Resource Materials | 111 |

# A FEW NOTES ABOUT THE AUTHOR
# ERNEST HEMINGWAY

HEMINGWAY, Ernest (1899-1961). A writer famous for his terse, direct style, Ernest Hemingway was also known for the way in which his own life mirrored the activities and interests of his characters. Many of his works show man pitted against nature, as in his favorite sports-hunting, fishing, and bullfighting. In others he tells of the experiences of wartime-man against man. The immediate appeal of his best writing probably stems from the fact that he wrote of things he knew intimately and that were important to him.

Ernest Hemingway was born on July 21, 1899, in Oak Park, Ill., a Chicago suburb. His father was a doctor. After high school Hemingway got a job as a reporter on the Kansas City Star. During World War I he tried to enlist in the armed forces but was rejected because of an old eye injury. He volunteered as an ambulance driver on the Italian front, and in 1918 he was badly wounded.

After the war he settled in Paris, France, where he began to write fiction. He submitted his work for criticism to the poet Ezra Pound and to Gertrude Stein, a writer who served as friend and adviser to many writers of the time. The first of many collections of stories, 'In Our Time', published in 1925, did not sell well. His novel 'The Sun Also Rises', which came out a year later, made his name known. It tells of young people in postwar Paris and their search for
values in a world that in many ways has lost its meaning.

In 'A Farewell to Arms' (1929), about war on the Italian front, Hemingway tells a love story that is interspersed with scenes of magnificent battle reporting. 'To Have and Have Not' (1937) shows Hemingway's interest in social problems, an interest more fully realized in 'For Whom the Bell Tolls' (1940), set in the Spanish Civil War. In 'Across the River and into the Trees' (1950) an army officer dies while on leave. This novel is generally considered inferior to 'The Old Man and the Sea' (1952), which won a Pulitzer prize in 1953. Hemingway received the Nobel prize for literature in 1954.

Hemingway was a war correspondent in Spain, China, and Europe during World War II. He was married four times and had three sons. Toward the end of his life he suffered from anxiety and depression. He died on July 2, 1961, in his home in Ketchum, Idaho, of a self-inflicted shotgun wound.


--- Courtesy of Compton's Learning Company

# INTRODUCTION

This unit has been designed to develop students' reading, writing, thinking, and language skills through exercises and activities related to *The Old Man and The Sea* by Ernest Hemingway. It includes eighteen lessons, supported by extra resource materials.

The **introductory lessons** introduce students to the themes of heroism and resolution through a film, discussion, and a bulletin board activity. Following the introductory activities, students are given a transition to explain how the activities relate to the book they are about to read. Following the transition, students are given the materials they will be using during the unit. At the end of the lesson, students begin the pre-reading work for the first reading assignment.

The **reading assignments** are approximately thirty pages each; some are a little shorter while others are a little longer. Students have approximately 15 minutes of pre-reading work to do prior to each reading assignment. This pre-reading work involves reviewing the study questions for the assignment and doing some vocabulary work for 8 to 10 vocabulary words they will encounter in their reading.

The **study guide questions** are fact-based questions; students can find the answers to these questions right in the text. These questions come in two formats: short answer required or multiple choice. The best use of these materials is probably to use the short answer version of the questions as study guides for students (since answers will be more complete), and to use the multiple choice version for occasional quizzes. If your school has the appropriate machinery, it might be a good idea to make transparencies of your answer keys for the overhead projector.

The **vocabulary work** is intended to enrich students' vocabularies as well as to aid in the students' understanding of the book. Prior to each reading assignment, students will complete a two-part worksheet for approximately 8 to 10 vocabulary words in the upcoming reading assignment. Part I focuses on students' use of general knowledge and contextual clues by giving the sentence in which the word appears in the text. Students are then to write down what they think the words mean based on the words' usage. Part II nails down the definitions of the words by giving students dictionary definitions of the words and having students match the words to the correct definitions based on the words' contextual usage. Students should then have a thorough understanding of the words when they meet them in the text.

After each reading assignment, students will go back and formulate answers for the study guide questions. Discussion of these questions serves as a **review** of the most important events and ideas presented in the reading assignments.

After students complete reading the work, a lesson is devoted to the **extra discussion questions/writing assignments**. These questions focus on interpretation, critical analysis and personal response, employing a variety of thinking skills and adding to the students' understanding of the novel.

Following the discussion questions, there is a **vocabulary review** lesson which pulls together all of the fragmented vocabulary lists for the reading assignments and gives students a review of all of the words they have studied.

The **group activity** which follows the discussion questions has students working in small groups to discuss the idea of heroism--what it means to be a hero and the characteristics of Hemingway's code hero. Using the information they have acquired so far through individual work and class discussions, students get together to further examine the text and to brainstorm ideas relating to this theme of the novel.

There are three **writing assignments** in this unit, each with the purpose of informing, persuading, or having students express personal opinions. The first assignment is to persuade: students pretend to be Manolin and try to persuade Santiago to go back home rather than remaining with the fish. The second assignment is to inform: following the nonfiction assignment, students write a composition about a topic related to *The Old Man and the Sea*. The third assignment is to give students a chance to reflect on their own lives and to express their own opinions: students write a composition entitled "But There Is Only One Me," (a take-off on Manolin's line about Santiago, "There are many good fisherman and some great ones. But there is only you.")

In addition, there is a **nonfiction reading assignment**. Students are required to read a piece of nonfiction related in some way to *The Old Man and The Sea* (articles about prejudice or coming of age, trial transcripts, etc.). After reading their nonfiction pieces, students will fill out a worksheet on which they answer questions regarding facts, interpretation, criticism, and personal opinions. During one class period, students make **oral presentations** about the nonfiction pieces they have read. This not only exposes all students to a wealth of information, it also gives students the opportunity to practice **public speaking**.

The **review lesson** pulls together all of the aspects of the unit. The teacher is given four or five choices of activities or games to use which all serve the same basic function of reviewing all of the information presented in the unit.

The **unit test** comes in two formats: all multiple choice-matching-true/false or with a mixture of matching, short answer, multiple choice, and composition. As a convenience, two different tests for each format have been included.

There are additional **support materials** included with this unit. The **extra activities section** includes suggestions for an in-class library, crossword and word search puzzles related to the novel, and extra vocabulary worksheets. There is a list of **bulletin board ideas** which gives the teacher suggestions for bulletin boards to go along with this unit. In addition, there is a list of **extra class activities** the teacher could choose from to enhance the unit or as a substitution for an exercise the teacher might feel is inappropriate for his/her class.

**Answer keys** are located directly after the **reproducible student materials** throughout the unit. The student materials may be reproduced for use in the teacher's classroom without infringement of copyrights. No other portion of this unit may be reproduced without the written consent of Teacher's Pet Publications, Inc.

The **level** of this unit can be varied depending upon the criteria on which the individual assignments are graded, the teacher's expectations of his/her students in class discussions, and the formats chosen for the study guides, quizzes and test. If teachers have other ideas/activities they wish to use, they can usually easily be inserted prior to the review lesson.

# UNIT OBJECTIVES - *The Old Man and the Sea*

1. Through reading Ernest Hemingway's *The Old Man and The Sea,* students will gain a better understanding of the "code hero" and Hemingway's views toward nature.

2. Students will be able to find and define the symbols used in *The Old Man and The Sea.*

3. Students will study the theme of the importance of resolution (determination) in reaching one's goals.

4. Students will demonstrate their understanding of the text on four levels: factual, interpretive, critical and personal.

5. Students will define their own viewpoints on the aforementioned themes.

6. Students will be given the opportunity to practice reading aloud and silently to improve their skills in each area.

7. Students will answer questions to demonstrate their knowledge and understanding of the main events and characters in *The Old Man and The Sea* as they relate to the author's theme development.

8. Students will enrich their vocabularies and improve their understanding of the novel through the vocabulary lessons prepared for use in conjunction with the novel.

9. The writing assignments in this unit are geared to several purposes:
    a. To have students demonstrate their abilities to inform, to persuade, or to express their own personal ideas
        Note: Students will demonstrate ability to write effectively to <u>inform</u> by developing and organizing facts to convey information. Students will demonstrate the ability to write effectively to <u>persuade</u> by selecting and organizing relevant information, establishing an argumentative purpose, and by designing an appropriate strategy for an identified audience. Students will demonstrate the ability to write effectively to <u>express personal ideas</u> by selecting a form and its appropriate elements.
    b. To check the students' reading comprehension
    c. To make students think about the ideas presented by the novel
    d. To encourage logical thinking
    e. To provide an opportunity to practice good grammar and improve students' use of the English language.

# READING ASSIGNMENTS - *Old Man and The Sea*

| Date Assigned | Pages | Completion Date |
|---|---|---|
|  |  |  |
|  |  |  |
|  |  |  |
|  |  |  |

## READING ASSIGNMENTS

Since there are no chapters marked in this relatively short novel, the reading assignments are divided by events. Page numbers vary according to the edition used, so quotations from the novel are used as beginning or ending points. On your reading assignment sheets you can fill in the exact page numbers from the books you are using.

Reading Assignment #1: Beginning to "Good Luck, Old Man" (when Santiago leaves for his fishing trip).

Reading Assignment #2: Beginning of the fishing trip to when the fish jumps. "He's coming up . . . . Come on hand. Please come on."

Reading Assignment #3: The fish's jump to the fish's death. End with, "The fish was silvery and still and floated with the waves."

Reading Assignment #4: Fish's death to the end of the novel.

Since these are relatively long reading assignments, we've tried to allow ample time for completion.

When you fill in the Reading Assignment Sheet, use page numbers from your text to make finding the assignments easier for your students.

# UNIT OUTLINE - *The Old Man and The Sea*

| 1 | 2 | 3 | 4 | 5 |
|---|---|---|---|---|
| Film | Film | Introduction "Hero" | PV&R 1 | Study ?s 1<br><br>PV&R 2 |
| **6**<br><br>Study ?s 2<br><br>Sentence Structure<br><br>P&V 3 | **7**<br><br>Read 3 | **8**<br><br>Study ?s 3<br><br>PV&R 4 | **9**<br><br>Study ?s 4<br><br>Discussion | **10**<br><br>Vocabulary |
| **11**<br><br>Writing Assignment #1 | **12**<br><br>Group Activity | **13**<br><br>Library | **14**<br><br>Nonfiction Reports | **15**<br><br>Writing Assignment #2 |
| **16**<br><br>Review | **17**<br><br>Test | **18**<br><br>Writing Assignment #3 | | |

Key:   P = Preview Study Questions   V = Prereading Vocabulary Work   R = Read

# STUDY GUIDE QUESTIONS

# SHORT ANSWER STUDY GUIDE QUESTIONS - *The Old Man and The Sea*

## Reading Assignment #1

1. Who is Santiago? Describe him.
2. Who is Manolin?
3. Identify Martin.
4. Why is the boy not fishing with the old man anymore? Does he want to?
5. What did the other fishermen think of the old man?
6. Describe Santiago's house.
7. What's the point behind the conversation about yellow rice with fish and the cast net?
8. Why is there so much talk about baseball, specifically DiMaggio?
9. "There are many good fishermen and some great ones. But there is only you." What does the boy mean?
10. What is Hemingway's point to having the old man say, "I may not be as strong as I think . . ."
11. What did the old man dream about?

## Reading Assignment #2

1. How did Santiago think of the sea? (To what does he compare it?)
2. "It is better to be lucky. But I would rather be exact. Then when luck comes, you are ready." Explain.
3. What fish did the old man catch first?
4. "If the other heard me talking out loud, they would think that I am crazy . . . But since I am not crazy, I do not care." What does that tell us about the old man's character?
5. What happened when the old man first tried to pull in the bill fish?
6. What does the old man think of porpoises and flying fish, and the pair of marlin he had hooked before?
7. Santiago often wishes the boy were there. Why?
8. "His choice had been to stay in the deep dark water far out beyond all snares and traps . . . My choice was to go there to find him beyond all people . . . in the world." Explain the importance of this passage.
9. Why did Santiago want the fish to turn and swim with the current?
10. Explain the significance of "Take a good rest, small bird . . . Then go in and take your chances like any man or bird or fish."
11. What happened when the fish lurched?
12. What was Santiago's problem with the left hand?

*Old Man* Short Answer Study Guide Questions Page 2

Reading Assignment #3
1. How big was the fish?
2. "But, thank God, they are not as intelligent as we who kill them, although they are more noble and more able." What's Hemingway saying?
3. "He settled comfortably against the wood and took his suffering as it came . . . " is one of the many religious references in the novel. To whom is Santiago compared in this one?
4. Santiago feels he must "prove himself" to the fish and to the boy. "Now he was proving it again. Each time was a new time . . . . " What is the implication in broader terms; do we EVER stop having to prove ourselves (according to Hemingway)?
5. Who was El Campeon? How did he get that name?
6. What second fish did the old man catch, and what will he do with it?
7. Santiago tries to justify killing the big fish by thinking of how many people he will feed. What does the old man conclude?
8. Santiago sleeps again. What does he dream of now?
9. What woke him up?
10. When did the fish start to circle?
11. How did the old man kill the big fish?

Reading Assignment #4
1. How did Santiago intend to take the fish back to port since the fish was bigger than the boat?
2. Santiago asks himself," . . . is he bringing me in or am I bringing him in?" What does he conclude?
3. What problem did the old man have getting the fish home?
4. What are the old man's arguments with himself about whether or not killing the big fish is a sin? (What arguments does he make for and against it being a sin?)
5. The old man apologizes to the big fish. ("I am sorry that I went too far out. I ruined us both.") Why?
6. What of the big fish is left by the time Santiago reaches home?
7. With the mast on his shoulder, Santiago had to stop and rest five times on his way home. What is the symbolic reference?
8. Identify Pedrico.
9. Why does Manolin cry?
10. What is the conclusion of the story?

# ANSWER KEY SHORT ANSWER STUDY GUIDE QUESTIONS - *The Old Man and The Sea*

Reading Assignment #1

1. Who is Santiago? Describe him.
   Santiago is the main character in the novel. He is an old man, gaunt and weather-worn with the many scars of an old fisherman.

2. Who is Manolin?
   Manolin is Santiago's friend, a boy who fished with Santiago before his streak of bad luck.

3. Identify Martin.
   Martin is the owner of a pub-type restaurant. He sent food with Manolin to Santiago.

4. Why is the boy not fishing with the old man anymore? Does he want to?
   Santiago is having a streak of very bad luck; he is not catching any fish. Manolin's parents won't let him fish with Santiago anymore even though he wants to.

5. What did the other fishermen think of the old man?
   Many fishermen made fun of the old man. Some of the older fishermen looked at him and were sad. No one would steal from him.

6. Describe Santiago's house.
   Santiago's house was small, had only the necessities for one old man's everyday life: a bed, a chair, a table, a place to cook on the dirt floor, some religious pictures, a picture of his deceased wife, and a clean shirt. The house was neat and clean.

7. What's the point behind the conversation about yellow rice with fish and the cast net?
   There was no yellow rice or cast net; this is a standing joke -- perhaps a wish -- between the two friends.

8. Why is there so much talk about baseball, specifically DiMaggio?
   Santiago's hero, Joe DiMaggio, was successful playing baseball even though the odds were against him. By identifying with DiMaggio, Santiago sees that success is sometimes possible (no matter what the odds) if you want it enough.

9. "There are many good fishermen and some great ones. But there is only you." What does the boy mean?
   Manolin means that the old man is special. One could also take it to mean that no matter what talents anyone else has, you have to use what you are given to accomplish the tasks in your own life.

10. What is Hemingway's point to having the old man say, "I may not be as strong as I think . . . . But I know many tricks and I have resolution"?
    Pure strength isn't the only important thing for a good fisherman to have. If one is smart and persistent, he can accomplish a great deal without tremendous strength.

11. What did the old man dream about?
    He dreamed of things he remembered from his youth in Africa and the lions on the beaches there.

Reading Assignment #2

1. How did Santiago think of the sea? (To what does he compare it?)
    Santiago compares the sea to a woman, as one that "gave or withheld great favours, and if she did wild or wicked things it was because she could not help them.

2. "It is better to be lucky. But I would rather be exact. Then when luck comes, you are ready." Explain.
    The old man prepared his fishing gear very carefully and did all he could to increase his chances of getting some fish. He made himself ready to take advantage of any lucky strike he might find, so he wouldn't have equipment failure or be lacking something he needed when he found fish.

3. What fish did the old man catch first?
    The old man caught a tuna first.

4. "If the other heard me talking out loud, they would think that I am crazy . . . But since I am not crazy, I do not care." What does that tell us about the old man's character?
    He knows himself and has self-confidence enough to not really care about what other people think.

5. What happened when the old man first tried to pull in the bill fish?
    The old man could not raise him an inch. The big fish towed the old man's boat.

6. What does the old man think of porpoises and flying fish, and the pair of marlin he had hooked before?
    Santiago thought of porpoises, flying fish and marlin as his brothers in the natural world.

7. Santiago often wishes the boy were there. Why?
    He liked the boy's company and really could use some help.

8. "His choice had been to stay in the deep dark water far out beyond all snares and traps . . . My choice was to go there to find him beyond all people . . . in the world." Explain the importance of this passage.
   Santiago has broken some unspoken law of nature by fishing beyond the normal fishing boundaries. The magnificent fish stayed within its natural, allotted environment. The old man trespassed and paid a high price for his "sin" against nature.

9. Why did Santiago want the fish to turn and swim with the current?
   The fish would swim with the current when it got tired. That would mean Santiago's battle would almost be over.

10. Explain the significance of "Take a good rest, small bird . . . Then go in and take your chances like any man or bird or fish."
    Santiago could offer the bird a safe resting place for a little while, but, in the end, the bird would have to fly on and take its chances for good luck or bad luck, life or death, just like all creatures do in nature.

11. What happened when the fish lurched?
    The fish pulled Santiago over in the boat. He fell on his face and got a cut below his eye. The second lurch caused a cut in Santiago's right hand.

12. What was Santiago's problem with the left hand?
    The left hand kept cramping.

Reading Assignment #3

1. How big was the fish?
   The fish was two feet longer than the skiff.

2. "But, thank God, they are not as intelligent as we who kill them, although they are more noble and more able." What's Hemingway saying?
   If the fish had man's intelligence with its own nobility and ability, Santiago thinks men wouldn't be able to catch fish.

3. "He settled comfortably against the wood and took his suffering as it came . . . " is one of the many religious references in the novel. To whom is Santiago compared in this one?
   The comparison could be to Christ's suffering while carrying the wooden cross.

4. Santiago feels he must "prove himself" to the fish and to the boy. "Now he was proving it again. Each time was a new time . . . . " What is the implication in broader terms; do we EVER stop having to prove ourselves (according to Hemingway)?
   If our past actions don't count for anything, and each new situation requires our best performance, then we must never stop proving ourselves.

5. Who was El Campeon? How did he get that name?
   El Campeon was Santiago, a champion arm wrestler in his youth. He beat a great athlete in an arm wrestling match. The point is that he broke the athlete's confidence; he was able to meet the other man's strength, and in a battle of perseverance, Santiago won.

6. What second fish did the old man catch, and what will he do with it?
   He caught a dolphin and saved it to eat later.

7. Santiago tries to justify killing the big fish by thinking of how many people he will feed. What does the old man conclude?
   No one is worthy to eat the noble fish.

8. Santiago sleeps again. What does he dream of now?
   He dreams of porpoises, that his right arm is asleep, and about the lions on the beach.

9. What woke him up?
   His hand hit him in the face as the big fish took the line and jumped.

10. When did the fish start to circle?
    The fish started to circle on the third morning of the fishing trip.

11. How did the old man kill the big fish?
    The old man pulled the fish close, got him turned on his side, held the line with his foot, and harpooned the big fish.

Reading Assignment #4

1. How did Santiago intend to take the fish back to port since the fish was bigger than the boat?
   Santiago tied the fish to the side of the skiff.

2. Santiago asks himself," . . . is he bringing me in or am I bringing him in?" What does he conclude?
   He decides they are bringing each other in. They are equals, side by side. Santiago is only better through "trickery," and the fish meant no harm.

3. What problem did the old man have getting the fish home?
   Sharks kept attacking the bloody carcass of the dead, big fish.

4. What are the old man's arguments with himself about whether or not killing the big fish is a sin? (What arguments does he make for and against it being a sin?)
   Santiago thinks it is not a sin to kill the fish because killing the fish will keep himself alive and feed many people. He thinks he was born to be a fisherman and the fish was born to be a fish. Then, he thinks it _is_ a sin because he killed the fish out of pride more than necessity and because he loved the fish. Then, he rationalizes that "everything kills everything else in some way."

5. The old man apologizes to the big fish. ("I am sorry that I went too far out. I ruined us both.") Why?
   The old man sees the once noble fish now mutilated, lifeless, and defenseless against the shark attacks, and Santiago feels truly sorry about that. One could conclude that by going "too far out," beyond the boundaries previously set by other fishermen, Santiago has tampered with nature. In doing so, he has not only destroyed the magnificent fish, he also has lost a great deal himself.

6. What of the big fish is left by the time Santiago reaches home?
   Only the carcass is left: the tail, the backbone, the head and bill.

7. With the mast on his shoulder, Santiago had to stop and rest five times on his way home. What is the symbolic reference?
   Again, there is a reference to Christ's carrying the cross.

8. Identify Pedrico.
   Pedrico looked after the old man's skiff and gear and received the head of the big fish from the old man.

9. Why does Manolin cry?
   Manolin cries for the old man's suffering and defeat.

10. What is the conclusion of the story?
    A woman and her husband see the carcass of the magnificent fish and incorrectly identify it as a common shark of extraordinary size. This emphasizes the fall of the noble creature and the apparent insignificance of Santiago's great sin and battle in the everyday lives of other people. At the end of the story, Santiago himself is sleeping, dreaming once again of the lions on the beaches of Africa.

# MULTIPLE CHOICE STUDY GUIDE/QUIZ QUESTIONS - *The Old Man and The Sea*

Reading Assignment #1

1. Who is Santiago? How is he described in the story?
    a. He is the ship's captain. He is tall and muscular and looks almost arrogant.
    b. He is the richest man in the village. He is short, but carries himself proudly, so that he looks tall. He has a birthmark on one side of his face.
    c. He is one of the business men who buys the fish. He has a greasy, dishonest look about him.
    d. He is the old fisherman. he is gaunt and weather-worn with many scars.

2. Who is Manolin?
    a. Manolin is Santiago's younger brother who is going to take over the fishing chores.
    b. Manolin is the leader of the village. He is trying to get Santiago to stop fishing.
    c. Manolin is Santiago's son who doesn't want to be a fisherman.
    d. Manolin is a young boy who often fishes with Santiago.

3. Identify Martin.
    a. Martin is the teacher in the village. He is trying to convince the people to try new ways.
    b. Martin is the owner of a pub-type restaurant. He sent food with Manolin to Santiago.
    c. Martin is the most successful fisherman in the village. He doesn't want any competition from Santiago.
    d. Martin is the doctor who is trying to convince Santiago to rest more because of his poor health.

4. Why is the boy not fishing with the old man anymore? Does he want to?
    a. Santiago is having a streak of bad luck. The boy's parents won't let him fish with Santiago even though he wants to.
    b. The boy has been offered a better paying job by one of the businessmen.
    c. The boy has had an accident while fishing. he is recuperating.
    d. Santiago and the boy had a fight because the boy was stealing fish. Santiago refused to take him fishing anymore.

5. What did the other fishermen think of the old man?
    a. They thought he was a good example of the virtues of hard work and honest living. They encouraged their sons to emulate him.
    b. They thought he was just a crazy old man and they ignored him.
    c. They felt sad and sorry for him. No one would steal from him.
    d. They thought he was possessed by an evil spirit. They were afraid to go near him and also kept their families away.

*Old Man* Multiple Choice Study Guide Page 2

6. Describe Santiago's house.
    a. It was large, but in a state of disrepair because he couldn't afford to fix it.
    b. It was small and had only the necessities for the old man's everyday life. It was neat and clean.
    c. It was not a typical house. He brought the boat up on the beach at night, put a tarpaulin over it, and slept in the bottom of the boat.
    d. It was of average size for the village with comfortable furniture. he had left everything the way his dead wife had arranged it.

7. What's the point behind the conversation about yellow rice with fish and the cast net?
    a. It is a repetition of the first conversation they ever had.
    b. It foreshadows Santiago's later good fortune.
    c. It shows that Manolin really has a double personality; he is outwardly kind but inwardly mean.
    d. It is a joke or perhaps a wish between the two friends. There really is no rice or net.

8. Why is there so much talk about baseball, specifically Joe DiMaggio?
    a. Santiago identifies with DiMaggio, and sees that success is sometimes possible, no matter what the odds, if you want it enough.
    b. Baseball was the fishermen's only means of escape from the harshness of their existence.
    c. Santiago and the other men in the village had pooled their small savings and bet on DiMaggio's team to win. They listened to the games, hoping to become rich.
    d. DiMaggio's ancestors were from the village where Santiago lived. Santiago had known DiMaggio's grandfather when they were boys. The people of the village felt a personal kinship with him.

9. "There are many good fishermen and some great ones. But there is only you." What does the boy mean?
    a. It is a thinly disguised insult. Manolin has lost faith in Santiago.
    b. Manolin doesn't want to tell Santiago outright that he is really too old to be out fishing, so he tries to make subtle hints.
    c. Manolin means that Santiago is special. It could also mean that one has to use the talents one is given in life.
    d. He means that experience is the best teacher.

*Old Man* Multiple Choice Study Guide Page 3

10. What is Hemingway's point to having the old man say, "I may not be as strong as I think . . . But I know many tricks and I have resolution?"
    a. He is telling the other fishermen that he doesn't want their help or their pity.
    b. Hemingway wants to make sure the readers fully understand the fisherman's character and motivations.
    c. Santiago is insulting the other fishermen, telling them that he is much wiser and more experienced. He is bitter because they don't respect him.
    d. Pure strength isn't the only important thing for a fisherman to have. If one is smart and persistent, he can accomplish great things without tremendous strength.

11. What did the old man dream about?
    a. He dreamed about his wife and his early married life.
    b. He dreamed about his youth in Africa and lions on the beach there.
    c. He dreamed about living in a big house with beautiful gardens.
    d. He dreamed about going to New York to see Joe DiMaggio and the Yankees play.

*Old Man* Multiple Choice Study Guide Page 4

Reading Assignment #2

12. How did Santiago think of the sea?
    a. He compares the sea to a woman who could give or withhold great favors, and sometimes did wild or wicked things.
    b. He compared it to a baseball team that could either be calm or excited and angry.
    c. He compared it to the mouth of a huge fish that could swallow a man whole and spit him out again.
    d. He compared it to a temperamental, child-like god who never rested.

13. "It is better to be lucky. But I would rather be exact. Then when luck comes, you are ready." Explain.
    a. Good luck takes less work than exactness and yields better rewards.
    b. He knows that he has bad luck, so he is defending himself by saying that he prefers the other qualities.
    c. He made himself ready to take advantage of any lucky strike he might have by carefully preparing his fishing gear.
    d. Santiago believes that God will ultimately reward his patience and faith.

14. What fish did the old man catch first?
    a. He caught a dolphin.
    b. He caught a tuna.
    c. He caught a swordfish.
    d. He caught a bluefish.

15. "If the other heard me talking out loud, they would think that I am crazy . . . But since I am not crazy, I do not care." What does that tell us about the old man's character?
    a. He knows himself and has the confidence not to care about what other people think.
    b. He is so out of touch that he doesn't realize he does things that seem crazy to others.
    c. He does not like the others so he deliberately does things to ostracize himself.
    d. He is really preoccupied with worrying about what the others think although he will not admit it.

16. What happened when the old man first tried to pull in the bill fish?
    a. The line got caught around the fish's tail.
    b. He got a rope burn.
    c. The fish towed the old man's boat with him.
    d. The hook sank deeper into the fish's mouth.

*Old Man* Multiple Choice Study Guide Page 5

17. What does the old man think of porpoises and flying fish, and the pair of marlin he had hooked before?
    a. Santiago thought of them as inferior and not worthy of his great skill.
    b. He thinks of them only as food and money.
    c. He thinks of them as obstructions to be overcome.
    d. He thinks of them as brothers in the natural world.

18. Santiago often wishes the boy were there. Why?
    a. He is afraid that he is going to die alone and no one will ever find his body.
    b. He likes Manolin's company and needs the help.
    c. Manolin can read the sports pages to him to pass the time while they are waiting for the fish to tire.

19. "His choice had been to stay in the deep dark water far out beyond all snares and traps . . . My choice was to go there to find him beyond all people . . . in the world." Explain the importance of this passage.
    a. Santiago admits that the fish is wiser and more powerful than he is.
    b. Santiago is regretting that he ever went out after the fish. He realizes that he should have listened to the others.
    c. Santiago feels almost god-like in his capture and probable domination of the fish.
    d. Santiago has broken an unspoken law of nature and will pay a high price for his sin.

20. Why did Santiago want the fish to turn and swim with the current?
    a. It would bring Santiago within the range of other boats and he could get help.
    b. He was afraid that if they went further out to sea he would never get back.
    c. The fish would swim with the current when it got tired. That would mean that Santiago's battle would be almost over.
    d. Santiago wanted to attract even bigger fish, and thought there was more likelihood of that if he were going with the current.

21. Explain the significance of "Take a good rest, small bird . . . Then go in and take your chances like any man or bird or fish."
    a. If Santiago didn't catch the fish soon, he would kill and eat the bird.
    b. The bird could be safe with Santiago for a while, but would then have to fly on with his life, as all creatures must do.
    c. Santiago is getting deranged. He thinks the bird can understand him. This shows us his deteriorating mental and physical state.
    d. Santiago is really wishing he could take a rest, and that the bird could somehow help him.

*Old Man* Multiple Choice Study Guide Page 6

22. What happened when the fish lurched?
    a. The fish pulled Santiago over in the boat. He fell on his face and got a cut below his eye. The second lurch caused a cut in Santiago's right hand.
    b. Santiago dislocated his shoulder and was in great pain.
    c. The lurching motion caused one oar to fall overboard. Santiago fell out of the boat trying to retrieve it, and strained his back while climbing back into the boat.
    d. The rope got caught around Santiago's leg. The fish pulled so hard that the rope broke Santiago's leg.

23. What was Santiago's problem with the left hand?
    a. He had broken three of the fingers.
    b. It was paralyzed.
    c. It kept cramping.
    d. It was trembling so much he couldn't use it.

*Old Man* Multiple Choice Study Guide Page 7

Reading Assignment #3

24. How big was the fish?
    a. It was half as long as the skiff.
    b. It was 35 feet long.
    c. It was twice the size of the skiff.
    d. It was two feet longer than the skiff.

25. "But, thank God, they are not as intelligent as we who kill them, although they are more noble and more able."  What's Hemingway saying?
    a. If the fish had man's intelligence with its own nobility and ability, Santiago thinks men wouldn't be able to catch the fish.
    b. We shouldn't kill creatures that are not as smart as we are.
    c. God made the lower creatures less intelligent so we could catch them more easily.
    d. We are intelligent, but not intelligent enough to stop killing. This makes the lower animals more noble.

26. "He settled comfortably against the wood and took his suffering as it came . . . " is one of the many religious references in the novel.  To whom is Santiago compared in this one?
    a. He is compared to St. Joseph.
    b. He is compared to Christ.
    c. He is compared to St. Peter the fisherman.
    d. He is compared to St. John.

27. Santiago feels he must "prove himself" to the fish and to the boy. "Now he was proving it again. Each time was a new time . . . . " What is the implication in broader terms; do we EVER stop having to prove ourselves (according to Hemingway)?
    a. Once we have accomplished a task to our best ability we can stop proving ourselves.
    b. We can never do anything perfectly, so it is a waste of time to keep proving ourselves.
    c. If our past actions don't count for anything, and each new situation requires our best performance, then we must never stop proving ourselves.
    d. Since no one else's opinion really counts, we must each make the individual decision whether or not to prove ourselves to ourselves.

*Old Man* Multiple Choice Study Guide Page 8

28. Who was El Campeon? How did he get that name?
    a. El Campeon was Santiago, as champion arm wrestler in his youth. He beat a great athlete in an arm wrestling match.
    b. It was a title that went each year to the fisherman in the village who had caught the most fish. Santiago had never achieved it.
    c. It was the nickname Santiago used when he referred to the pitcher of the Yankees. Santiago thought he was the best pitcher in the league.
    d. He was a prize winning bull fighter. He was also Santiago's brother who had left the village as a young boy and made a name for himself.

29. What second fish did the old man catch, and what will he do with it?
    a. He caught an ocean perch and used it as bait.
    b. He caught a swordfish and ate it immediately.
    c. He caught a sea bass and saved it as a gift for Manolin.
    d. He caught a dolphin and saved it to eat later.

30. Santiago tries to justify killing the big fish by thinking of how many people he will feed. What does the old man conclude?
    a. He would only feed the children of the village.
    b. He would share it equally among all of the villagers.
    c. He would not feed anyone; they were not worthy of eating it.
    d. He and Manolin would be the only ones, since he caught it.

31. Santiago sleeps again. What does he dream of now?
    a. He dreams again of his wife and their life together.
    b. He dreams of porpoises, that his right hand is asleep, and of lions on the beach.
    c. He dreams of the things he will buy with the money from the fish.
    d. He dreams of his upcoming battle with the great fish.

32. What woke him up?
    a. His hand hit him in the face as the big fish took the line and jumped.
    b. The smell of the dolphin rotting in the boat woke him.
    c. A wave washed over the boat and doused him with cold water.
    d. A group of sea gulls attacked the dolphin.

33. When did the fish start to circle?
    a. On the afternoon of the second day
    b. On the morning of the fourth day
    c. On the morning of the third day
    d. On the afternoon of the fifth day

*Old Man* Multiple Choice Study Guide Page 9

34. How did the old man kill the big fish?
    a. He shot it through the head with the only bullet he had left in his rifle.
    b. He let the fish run until it died of exhaustion.
    c. He managed to keep enough of the body out of the water that it died from lack of oxygen and exposure to the sun.
    d. He pulled the fish close, got him turned on his side, held the line with his foot, and harpooned it.

Reading Assignment #4

35. How did Santiago intend to take the fish back to port since the fish was bigger than the boat?
    a. He tied the fish to the side of the skiff.
    b. He towed it behind the skiff.
    c. He cut it up and put the pieces in the boat.
    d. He cut the fish in three equal pieces, tied one to the rear and one to each side of the boat.

36. Santiago asks himself," . . . is he bringing me in or am I bringing him in?" What does he conclude?
    a. He is bringing in the fish since he is the more intelligent of the two. His skill and determination, combined with his intelligence, have made him the victor.
    b. Neither is bringing in the other; it is the forces of nature at work on both of them.
    c. They are bringing each other in, as they are equals. Santiago is only better through trickery, and the fish meant no harm.
    d. The fish is bringing him in. The fish has won because he has injured Santiago.

37. What problem did the old man have getting the fish home?
    a. It was so heavy that the boat almost capsized because of the extra weight.
    b. Sharks kept attacking the bloody carcass.
    c. The sun was rotting the meat very quickly, and the smell was making Santiago sick.
    d. He kept falling asleep from exhaustion.

38. What are the old man's arguments with himself about whether or not killing the big fish is a sin? (What arguments does he make for and against it being a sin?)
    a. He argues about whether to share the profits from the fish or keep all of the money for himself.
    b. He argues about whether to use the fish as food for the villagers or to sell it to the fish brokers for profit.
    c. He argues about whether or not to abandon the fish's carcass in the water, since it is rapidly deteriorating anyway and since he has the knowledge of his victory.
    d. He argues about whether or not it is a sin to kill the fish.

*Old Man* Multiple Choice Study Guide Page 10

39. Santiago makes one last gesture to the fish on the journey home. What is it?
    a. He prays for the fish.
    b. He sings the traditional village mourning songs.
    c. He apologizes for killing it.
    d. He laughs and cheers out loud for his victory.

40. What of the big fish is left by the time Santiago reaches home?
    a. Nothing is left. The sharks have eaten everything including the bones.
    b. Only the carcass is left: the tail, the backbone, the head, and the bill.
    c. About half of the fish is left; enough to earn Santiago some money.
    d. Most of the fish is still there. Santiago managed to keep the sharks away and save it.

41. With the mast on his shoulder, Santiago had to stop and rest five times on his way home. What is the symbolic reference?
    a. It refers to Christ's carrying the cross.
    b. It refers to a soldier coming home from war.
    c. It refers to man's triumph over nature.
    d. It refers to the five decades Santiago has spent as a fisherman.

42. Identify Pedrico.
    a. He looked after the old man's skiff and gear and received the head of the big fish.
    b. He was the ringleader of the men who made fun of Santiago. The others turned away from him when they saw Santiago's fish.
    c. He was Manolin's younger brother who now wants to learn to fish with Santiago.
    d. He is the head of the village who welcomes Santiago home.

43. What does Manolin do when he sees Santiago return?
    a. He yells at him for going out alone.
    b. He cheers because Santiago has been victorious.
    c. He cries for Santiago's suffering and defeat.
    d. He ridicules Santiago for doing such a foolhardy thing.

44. A woman and her husband see the carcass of the magnificent fish and incorrectly identify it as a common shark of extraordinary size. What does this emphasize?
    a. Man's inability to recognize greatness in others
    b. The fall of the noble creature and the apparent insignificance of Santiago's great sin and battle
    c. Man's inability to celebrate the good fortune of another
    d. The impossibility of man's trying to conquer nature

*Old Man* Multiple Choice Study Guide Page 11

45. What is Santiago doing at the end of the story?
    a. He is sleeping, dreaming of lions on the beaches of Africa.
    b. He is retelling the story of catching the fish to all of the villagers.
    c. He is getting his boat ready to go out again.
    d. He is making soup with the fins and tail of the fish.

# ANSWER KEY - MULTIPLE CHOICE STUDY/QUIZ QUESTIONS
*The Old Man and The Sea*

| RA #1 | RA #2 | RA #3 | RA #4 |
|---|---|---|---|
| 1. D | 12. A | 24. D | 35. A |
| 2. D | 13. C | 25. A | 36. C |
| 3. B | 14. B | 26. B | 37. B |
| 4. A | 15. A | 27. C | 38. D |
| 5. C | 16. C | 28. A | 39. C |
| 6. B | 17. D | 29. D | 40. B |
| 7. D | 18. B | 30. C | 41. A |
| 8. A | 19. D | 31. B | 42. A |
| 9. C | 20. C | 32. A | 43. C |
| 10. D | 21. B | 33. C | 44. B |
| 11. B | 22. A | 34. D | 45. A |
|  | 23. C |  |  |

# PREREADING VOCABULARY WORKSHEETS

# VOCABULARY - *The Old Man and The Sea*

Reading Assignment 1 Part I: Using Prior Knowledge and Contextual Clues

Below are the sentences in which the vocabulary words appear in the text. Read the sentence. Use any clues you can find in the sentence combined with your prior knowledge, and write what you think the underlined words mean on the lines provided.

1. The brown blotches of the <u>benevolent</u> skin cancer the sun brings from its reflection on the tropic sea were on his cheeks.

   _____

2. I can remember the tail slapping and banging and the <u>thwart</u> breaking and the noise of the clubbing.

   _____

3. He was too simple to wonder when he had <u>attained</u> <u>humility.</u>

   _____

   _____

4. I may not be as strong as I think . . . . But I know many tricks and I have <u>resolution</u>.

   _____

5. . . . the old man carried the mast with the <u>furled</u> sail on his shoulder.

   _____

Part II: Determining the Meaning

Match the vocabulary words to their dictionary definitions.

___ 1. benevolent         A. A seat across a boat on which a rower may sit
___ 2. thwart             B. Rolled up and secured to something
___ 3. attained           C. Firm determination
___ 4. humility           D. Gained as an objective; achieved
___ 5. resolution         E. Marked by meekness or modesty in behavior
___ 6. furled              F. Characterized by or suggestive of doing good.

Vocabulary - *The Old Man and The Sea* Reading Assignment 2

Part I: Using Prior Knowledge and Contextual Clues
    Below are the sentences in which the vocabulary words appear in the text. Read the sentence. Use any clues you can find in the sentence combined with your prior knowledge, and write what you think the underlined words mean on the lines provided.

1. He saw the phosphorescence of the Gulf weed in the water . . . .

_____

2. . . . there was a sudden deep of seven hundred fathoms where all sorts of fish congregated because of the swirl the current made. . . .

_____

3. One bait was down forty fathoms.

_____

4. He watched the flying fish burst out again and again and the ineffectual movements of the bird.

_____

5. . . . nothing showed on the surface of the water but . . . the purple, formalized, iridescent, gelatinous bladder of a Portuguese man of war floating close beside the boat.

_____

6. They were immune to its poison.

_____

7. He loved green turtles and hawk-bills . . . and he had a friendly contempt for the huge, stupid loggerheads . . . .

_____

8. The position actually was only somewhat less intolerable; but he thought of it as almost comfortable.

_____

9. It is humiliating before others to have a diarrhoea from ptomaine poisoning or to vomit from it.

_____

Vocabulary - *The Old Man and The Sea* Reading Assignment 2 Continued

Part II: Determining the Meaning

___ 7. phosphorescence     A. Producing a display of lustrous, rainbowlike colors
___ 8. congregated     B. Scorn; disparaging or haughty disdain
___ 9. fathoms     C. Lowering the pride, dignity or self-respect
___ 10. ineffectual     D. Not affected by a given influence; unresponsive
___ 11. iridescent     E. Emission of light without burning
___ 12. immune     F. Insufficient to produce a desired effect
___ 13. contempt     G. Unbearable
___ 14. intolerable     H. Gathered; assembled
___ 15. humiliating     I. Units of length equal to six feet

Vocabulary - *The Old Man and The Sea* Reading Assignment 3

Part I: Using Prior Knowledge and Contextual Clues

Below are the sentences in which the vocabulary words appear in the text. Read the sentence. Use any clues you can find in the sentence combined with your prior knowledge, and write what you think the underlined words mean on the lines provided.

1. His sword was . . . tapered like a rapier . . . .

_____

2. But I will show him what a man can do and what a man endures.

_____

3. Its jaws were working convulsively in quick bites against the hook . . .

_____

4. Also now I have gained on him in the question of sustenance.

_____

5. Her lightness prolongs both out suffering but it is my safety since he has great speed that he has never yet employed.

_____

6. Make yourself do it and devise some simple and sure way about the lines.

_____

7. He just felt a faint slackening of the pressure of the line and he commenced to pull on it gently with his right hand.

_____

8. On each calm placid turn the fish made he was gaining line . . . .

_____

Vocabulary - *The Old Man and The Sea* Reading Assignment 3 Continued

Part II: Determining the Meaning
  Match the vocabulary words to their dictionary definitions.

___ 16. rapier         A. Shaking or agitating violently with irregular and involuntary muscular contractions.
___ 17. endures        B. Calm; quiet
___ 18. convulsively   C. A light, sharp-pointed sword lacking a cutting edge and used only for thrusting
___ 19. sustenance     D. To form, plan, or arrange in one's mind; design or contrive
___ 20. prolongs       E. Began; started
___ 21. devise         F. Something, esp. food, that sustains life or health
___ 22. commenced      G. To lengthen in duration; protract
___ 23. placid         H. To carry on through despite hardships

Vocabulary - *The Old Man and The Sea* Reading Assignment 4

Part I: Using Prior Knowledge and Contextual Clues
　　Below are the sentences in which the vocabulary words appear in the text. Read the sentence. Use any clues you can find in the sentence combined with your prior knowledge, and write what you think the underlined words mean on the lines provided.

1. He hit it without hope but with and complete <u>malignancy</u>.

_____

2. He did not like to look at the fish anymore since he had been <u>mutilated</u>.

_____

3. He is not a <u>scavenger</u> nor just a moving appetite as some sharks are.

_____

4. You <u>violated</u> your luck when you went too far outside.

_____


Part II: Determining the Meaning
　　Match the vocabulary words to their dictionary definitions.

___ 24. malignancy　　　　A. An animal that feeds on decaying matter
___ 25. mutilated　　　　　B. Broke or disregarded
___ 26. scavenger　　　　　C. Something disposed to do evil; highly injurious
___ 27. violated　　　　　　D. Disfigured beyond repair

# ANSWER KEY - VOCABULARY
*The Old Man and The Sea*

| RA 1 | RA 2 | RA 3 | RA 4 |
|---|---|---|---|
| 1. F | 7. E | 16. C | 24. C |
| 2. A | 8. H | 17. H | 25. D |
| 3. D | 9. I | 18. A | 26. A |
| 4. E | 10. F | 19. F | 27. B |
| 5. C | 11. A | 20. G | |
| 6. B | 12. D | 21. D | |
| | 13. B | 22. E | |
| | 14. G | 23. B | |
| | 15. C | | |

# DAILY LESSONS

## LESSONS ONE AND TWO

Objectives
1. To set up a discussion of what it means to be a hero
2. To give students a visual representation of a hero
3. To give students a visual representation of determination to do something regardless of the obstacles

Activity
Show a video of *Romancing the Stone*.

Homework
Tell students to bring in a picture or poster of people they admire, people who are their heroes, for Lesson Three. (Tell students the day and date)

## LESSON THREE

Objectives
1. To make clear the connections between *Romancing the Stone* and *The Old Man and the Sea*
2. To discuss what it means to be a hero
3. To set up the idea that (as Santiago says) "resolution," and "tricks" (ingenuity) can help one accomplish one's goals even if one is lacking other talents, strength or power with which one could accomplish the goal more easily

Activity #1
Use the following questions to guide a discussion of the movie *Romancing the Stone*:

1. What were the characteristics of Jesse, the hero of Joan Wilder's books?
2. Compare Coulton to Jesse.
3. Using Joan, Coulton, and Jesse as a basis for your answer, explain what characteristics a hero should have.
4. What obstacles do Joan and Coulton have to overcome before they finally get and keep the stone? Be specific.)
5. How do they overcome each of the obstacles?
6. Are Joan and Coulton the best-equipped and most powerful of the people searching for the stone? Why are they able to win in the end?

Activity #2
Tell students to take out the pictures of their heroes they were supposed to bring to class. Have each student tell about his picture and post it on the bulletin board you have prepared with the title: DID I EVER TELL YOU YOU'RE MY HERO? Using a marker write the characteristics of these heroes around the pictures.

# LESSON FOUR

## Objectives
1. To distribute the materials to be used in this unit
2. To preview the study questions for the first reading assignment
3. To preview the vocabulary for the first reading assignment
4. To read Reading Assignment 1

## Transition
"You have seen *Romancing the Stone* and have discussed some characteristics of heroes. The book you are going to read is about one man who wasn't a flashy hero like Jesse; nevertheless, he was one of Hemingway's code heroes. That is, a person who lived his life by a code, a set of values, and stuck by them through thick and thin. Like Joan and Coulton he has a firm determination to complete the task he has begun regardless of the risks or chances for success.

## Activity #1
Distribute the materials students will use in this unit. Explain in detail how students are to use these materials.

<u>Study Guides</u>  Students should read the study guide questions for each reading assignment prior to beginning the reading assignment to get a feeling for what events and ideas are important in the section they are about to read. After reading the section, students will (as a class or individually) answer the questions to review the important events and ideas from that section of the book. Students should keep the study guides as study materials for the unit test.

<u>Vocabulary</u>  Prior to reading a reading assignment, students will do vocabulary work related to the section of the book they are about to read. Following the completion of the reading of the book, there will be a vocabulary review of all the words used in the vocabulary assignments. Students should keep their vocabulary work as study materials for the unit test.

<u>Reading Assignment Sheet</u>  You need to fill in the reading assignment sheet to let students know by when their reading has to be completed. You can either write the assignment sheet up on a side blackboard or bulletin board and leave it there for students to see each day, or you can "ditto" copies for each student to have. In either case, you should advise students to become very familiar with the reading assignments so they know what is expected of them.

Extra Activities Center   The Extra Activities section of this unit contains suggestions for an extra library of related books and articles in your classroom as well as crossword and word search puzzles.  Make an extra activities center in your room where you will keep these materials for students to use. (Bring the books and articles in from the library and keep several copies of the puzzles on hand.) Explain to students that these materials are available for students to use when they finish reading assignments or other class work early.

Nonfiction Assignment Sheet   Explain to students that they each are to read at least one non-fiction piece from the in-class library at some time during the unit. Students will fill out a nonfiction assignment sheet after completing the reading to help you evaluate their reading experiences and to help the students think about and evaluate their own reading experiences.

Books   Each school has its own rules and regulations regarding student use of school books. Advise students of the procedures that are normal for your school.

Activity #2
   Give students about 15 minutes to preview the study questions and have students do the vocabulary work for Reading Assignment 1 of *The Old Man and The Sea*.

Activity #3
   Read Reading Assignment 1 orally in class. You probably know the best way to get readers with your class; pick students at random, ask for volunteers, or use whatever method works best for your group. If you have not yet completed an oral reading evaluation for your students this marking period, this would be a good opportunity to do so. A form is included with this unit for your convenience.

   If students do not complete this reading assignment in class, they should do so prior to your next class meeting.

# ORAL READING EVALUATION - *Old Man and the Sea*

Name _____ Class____ Date _____

| SKILL | EXCELLENT | GOOD | AVERAGE | FAIR | POOR |
|---|---|---|---|---|---|
| Fluency | 5 | 4 | 3 | 2 | 1 |
| Clarity | 5 | 4 | 3 | 2 | 1 |
| Audibility | 5 | 4 | 3 | 2 | 1 |
| Pronunciation | 5 | 4 | 3 | 2 | 1 |
| _____ | 5 | 4 | 3 | 2 | 1 |
| _____ | 5 | 4 | 3 | 2 | 1 |

Total _____ Grade _____

Comments:

# LESSON FIVE

Objectives
    1. To review the main ideas and events from Reading Assignment 1
    2. To preview the study questions and vocabulary for Reading Assignment 2
    3. To read Reading Assignment 2
    4. To evaluate students' oral reading


Activity #1

    Give students a few minutes to formulate answers for the study guide questions for Reading Assignment 1, and then discuss the answers to the questions in detail. Write the answers on the board or overhead transparency so students can have the correct answers for study purposes. Note: It is a good practice in public speaking and leadership skills for individual students to take charge of leading the discussions of the study questions. Perhaps a different student could go to the front of the class and lead the discussion each day that the study questions are discussed during this unit. Of course, the teacher should guide the discussion when appropriate and be sure to fill in any gaps the students leave.


Activity #2

    Give students about fifteen minutes to preview the study questions for Reading Assignment 2 of *The Old Man and The Sea* and to do the related vocabulary work.


Activity #3

    Choose students to read Reading Assignment 2 orally in class. Continue the oral reading evaluations. If students do not finish reading this assignment in class, they should do so independently prior to your next class period.

# LESSON SIX

## Objectives
1. To check to see that students finished Reading Assignment 2 as assigned
2. To review the main ideas and events from Reading Assignment 2
3. To preview the study questions for Reading Assignment 3
4. To familiarize students with the vocabulary in Reading Assignment 3
5. To look more closely at Hemingway's writing style
6. To review and practice types of sentence structure

## Activity #1
Quiz - Distribute quizzes and give students about 10 minutes to complete them. (Note: The quizzes may either be the short answer study guides or the multiple choice version for Reading Assignment 2.) Have students exchange papers. Grade the quizzes as a class. Collect the papers for recording the grades. (If you used the multiple choice version as a quiz, take a few minutes to discuss the answers for the short answer version if your students are using the short answer version for their study guides.)

## Activity #2
Tell students that professors, teachers and comedians all over the world have poked fun at Hemingway's "simple" writing style. He is well known for (among other things) his simple, declarative sentences as well as his use of "and" and "but." Write the following sentence on the board: "I don't know what fish that was that took the bait just now. It could have been a marlin or a broadbill or a shark. I never felt him. I had to get rid of him too fast."

If your students have skills in grammar, review many of the ways clauses and phrases can be put together by diagramming the sentence on the board and the several alternate sentences noted below.

If your students do not have skills in grammar (enough to understand clauses, phrases and modification), simply ask students to find different ways of saying the same information that is in the sentence on the board. Write down their responses.

Explain that there are many ways to structure sentences; a great deal depends on the individual's writing style and the effect he wishes to achieve. For example:

1. Just now, a fish took the bait. I don't know what kind it was; it could have been a marlin, a broadbill or a shark. Because I had to get rid of him too fast, I never felt him.

2. A fish just took the bait. I don't know what kind it was. It may have been a marlin. Maybe it was a broadbill or a shark. Having to get rid of him fast, I didn't feel him.

3. I don't know whether the fish that just took the bait was a marlin, a broadbill or a shark. I had to get rid of him before I could feel him.

4. Having to get rid of the fish that just took the bait, I couldn't feel whether he was a marlin, a broadbill or a shark.

There are many more ways these sentences could be rewritten. Explore more possibilities if you choose to do so.

Activity #3
Write these sentences on the board or make a transparency of them to put on the overhead projector. Have students rewrite each of them in at least three ways different from the author's version:

1. "It was cold now in the time before daylight and he pushed against the wood to be warm. I can do it as long as he can, he thought. And in the first light the line extended out and down into the water. The boat moved steadily and when the first edge of the sun rose it was on the old man's right shoulder."

2. "After a while the fish stopped beating at the wire and started circling slowly again. The old man was gaining line steadily now. But he felt faint again. He lifted some sea water with his left hand and put it on his head. Then he put more on and rubbed back of his neck."

3. "They sat on the terrace and many of the fishermen made fun of the old man and he was not angry. Others, of the older fishermen, looked at him and were sad. But they did not show it and they spoke politely about the current and the depths they had drifted their lives at and the steady good weather and of what they had seen."

Activity #4
Give students about 15 minutes to preview the study questions for Reading Assignment 3 and to do the related vocabulary work. If students do not finish this prior to the end of class, they should do so prior to your next class period.

## LESSON SEVEN

Objectives
    1. To read Reading Assignment 3
    2. To complete the oral reading evaluations

Activity

    Choose students to read Reading Assignment 3 orally in class. If students do not complete reading this section in class, they should do so prior to the next class period.

## LESSON EIGHT

Objectives
    1. To review the main ideas and events from Reading Assignment 3
    2. To preview the study questions and vocabulary for Reading Assignment 4
    3. To read Reading Assignment 4
    4. To evaluate students' oral reading

Activity #1

    Give students a few minutes to formulate answers for the study guide questions for Reading Assignment 3, and then discuss the answers to the questions in detail. Write the answers on the board or overhead transparency so students can have the correct answers for study purposes.

Activity #2

    Give students about fifteen minutes to preview the study questions for Reading Assignment 4 of *The Old Man and The Sea* and to do the related vocabulary work.

Activity #3

    Choose students to read Reading Assignment 4 orally in class. Continue the oral reading evaluations. If students do not finish reading this assignment in class, they should do so independently prior to your next class period.

# LESSON NINE

## Objectives

1. To review the main ideas and events from chapters 26-31
2. To discuss *The Old Man and The Sea* on interpretive and critical levels

## Activity #1

Take a few minutes at the beginning of the period to review the study questions for chapters 26-31.

## Activity #2

Choose the questions from the Extra Discussion Questions/Writing Assignments which seem most appropriate for your students. A class discussion of these questions is most effective if students have been given the opportunity to formulate answers to the questions prior to the discussion. To this end, you may either have all the students formulate answers to all the questions, divide your class into groups and assign one or more questions to each group, or you could assign one question to each student in your class. The option you choose will make a difference in the amount of class time needed for this activity.

## Activity #3

After students have had ample time to formulate answers to the questions, begin your class discussion of the questions and the ideas presented by the questions. Be sure students take notes during the discussion so they have information to study for the unit test.

# EXTRA WRITING ASSIGNMENTS/DISCUSSION QUESTIONS
## *The Old Man and The Sea*

<u>Interpretation</u>
1. Make a list of events in the story and place them into groups of events which seem to belong together. Explain why you have chosen the arrangement, and give each "chapter" a title.

2. If The *Old Man And The Sea* had been written only in the first person (if the old man were a narrator and our only source of information), how would that have changed the story and its effect?

3. Is the story of *The Old Man and the Sea* believable? Explain why or why not.

4. What does the setting add to the story? Why was it not set in a modern port?

5. Are the characters in *The Old Man And The Sea* stereotypes? If so, explain the usefulness of employing stereotypes in *The Old Man And The Sea*. If they are not, explain how they merit individuality.

6. The *Old Man And The Sea* is a very short novel. Could anything have been gained by including more scenes from the time before or after the events of the story? If so, what could have been added and for what purpose? If not, explain why not.

7. What are the conflicts in the story and how are they resolved?

<u>Critical</u>
8. Explain why the old man goes for the fish and stays with it until he brings the carcass to port even though he put himself at great risk to do so.

9. Describe Hemingway's writing style.

10. Compare Santiago to the marlin.

11. Compare and contrast Santiago and DiMaggio.

12. What function does the character of Manolin serve in the novel?

13. List several religious references in the story and explain why Hemingway chose this imagery.

14. Does Santiago undergo any type of change during the story? If so, what? If not, give possible reasons why he does not.

15. Explore the idea of nobility in the story.

*Old Man* Extra Questions Page 2

Personal Response

16. Suppose Santiago would tell about the events of this story a few years after it happened. What do you think he would say?

17. Would you like to be a fisherman like Santiago? Explain why or why not.

18. Why is this story titled *The Old Man and the Sea* instead of *The Old Man and the Fish*?

19. Will Santiago go after a big fish again? Explain why or why not.

20. A great deal of the book is spent describing in detail the old man's fight with the fish: an emotional and physical battle of almost epic proportions. Yet, when the old man returns, the whole experience is trivialized by the woman and her male companion, and life goes on pretty much as usual. This profound experience seems to have no profound consequences. Why not?

## LESSON TEN

Objective
> To review all of the vocabulary work done in this unit

Activity
> Choose one (or more) of the vocabulary review activities listed below and spend your class period as directed in the activity. Some of the materials for these review activities are located in the Vocabulary Resources section of this unit.

### VOCABULARY REVIEW ACTIVITIES

1. Divide your class into two teams and have an old-fashioned spelling or definition bee.

2. Give each of your students (or students in groups of two, three or four) a *The Old Man and The Sea* Vocabulary Word Search Puzzle. The person (group) to find all of the vocabulary words in the puzzle first wins.

3. Give students a *The Old Man and The Sea* Vocabulary Word Search Puzzle without the word list. The person or group to find the most vocabulary words in the puzzle wins.

4. Use a *The Old Man and The Sea* Vocabulary Crossword Puzzle. Put the puzzle onto a transparency on the overhead projector (so everyone can see it), and do the puzzle together as a class.

5. Give students a *The Old Man and The Sea* Vocabulary Matching Worksheet to do.

6. Divide your class into two teams. Use the *Old Man and The Sea* vocabulary words with their letters jumbled as a word list. Student 1 from Team A faces off against Student 1 from Team B. You write the first jumbled word on the board. The first student (1A or 1B) to unscramble the word wins the chance for his/her team to score points. If 1A wins the jumble, go to student 2A and give him/her a definition. He/she must give you the correct spelling of the vocabulary word which fits that definition. If he/she does, Team A scores a point, and you give student 3A a definition for which you expect a correctly spelled matching vocabulary word. Continue giving Team A definitions until some team member makes an incorrect response. An incorrect response sends the game back to the jumbled-word face off, this time with students 2A and 2B. Instead of repeating giving definitions to the first few students of each team, continue with the student after the one who gave the last incorrect response on the team. For example, if Team B wins the jumbled-word face-off, and student 5B gave the last incorrect answer for Team B, you would start this round of definition questions with student 6B, and so on. The team with the most points wins!

7. Have students write a story in which they correctly use as many vocabulary words as possible. Have students read their compositions orally! Post the most original compositions on your bulletin board!

# LESSON ELEVEN

Objectives
1. To give students the opportunity to practice writing to persuade
2. To check students' understanding of Santiago's motivations
3. To give the teacher the opportunity to evaluate students' writing skills

Activity

Distribute Writing Assignment #1. Discuss the directions in detail and give students ample time to complete the assignment.

Follow-Up: After you have graded the assignments, have a writing conference with the students. (This unit schedules one in Lesson Fifteen.) After the writing conference, allow students to revise their papers using your suggestions and corrections. Give them about three days from the date they receive their papers to complete the revision. I suggest grading the revisions on an A-C-E scale (all revisions well-done, some revisions made, few or no revisions made). This will speed your grading time and still give some credit for the students' efforts.

# LESSON TWELVE

Objectives
1. To investigate the text for characteristics of Santiago to determine characteristics of Hemingway's "code hero."
2. To have students work together in small groups to improve their group interaction skills and accomplish Objective 1.
3. Students will report their findings during a follow-up group discussion.

Activity #1

Divide the class into groups of four students. Explain that students are to work together to find characteristics of Santiago in order to determine the characteristics of Hemingway's "code hero."

Each of the four students in the group should investigate one section of the novel (most easily defined by the reading assignment divisions). Each should jot down the characteristics of Santiago he can find in his section along with examples where appropriate. Students will then compare and share notes, working together to compile a complete list of characteristics, which will be reported in Activity 2.

Activity #2

Have each group report its findings, giving the list of characteristics orally. Discuss the characteristics as necessary and make a list of the findings on the board for students to copy. Tell students to keep their lists and to be sure to bring them to Lesson Fifteen. (Give students a day and a date.)

# WRITING ASSIGNMENT #1 - *The Old Man and the Sea*

## PROMPT
For the purposes of this writing assignment, we are going to change the facts of the story a little bit. You are to pretend you are Manolin. You have gone out to sea with the old man on his quest for the big fish. You realize that the old man is practically killing himself for this fish. What would you say to persuade the old man to give up on the fish and go back home? Your assignment is to write a composition in which you persuade the old man to go back home.

## PREWRITING
One way to get started is to make a little list of all the reasons the old man is out there fighting the fish. Why is he there? What motivates him to stay there and endure the emotional and physical pain? Next, keeping these things in mind, make a little list of the arguments you could use to try to convince him to go back home. Now think of other things that might motivate him to go back home (besides things related to his reasons for staying with the fish). Jot them down.

Look at your list. Which single argument is your best, the most likely to convince Santiago to go back home? Put a star next to that one. Number the rest of your arguments in order from most persuasive to least persuasive.

## DRAFTING
Write your composition as if you were talking to Santiago. How would you bring up the subject of going home again? Use this as your introductory paragraph. The body of your composition will hold all of your best arguments. Start with a paragraph for your best argument. Then, write a paragraph for each of your other arguments. If you were talking to Santiago and had just told him all of these good reasons why he should go home, how would you finish your little speech? Use that for your concluding paragraph.

## PROMPT
When you finish the rough draft of your paper, ask a student who sits near you to read it. After reading your rough draft, he/she should tell you what he/she liked best about your work, which parts were difficult to understand, and ways in which your work could be improved. Reread your paper considering your critic's comments, and make the corrections you think are necessary.

## PROOFREADING
Do a final proofreading of your paper double-checking your grammar, spelling, organization, and the clarity of your ideas.

# LESSON THIRTEEN

<u>Objectives</u>
    1. To give students the opportunity to explore nonfiction topics related to the story
    2. To give students the opportunity to use the library
    3. To broaden students' knowledge of our world

<u>Activity</u>
    Take students to the library. Explain to them that this is their opportunity to complete the nonfiction reading assignment which accompanies this unit. Students are to find nonfiction books or articles in some way relating to *The Old Man and the Sea*. Students are to use this time to find nonfiction materials that interest them and to begin reading. Remind students to complete the Nonfiction Assignment Sheet after they have done their reading.

    Remind students that they will be giving a little oral report about their nonfiction reading in the next class period.

    Suggested Topics:
        Biography of Hemingway
        Articles about *The Old Man and the Sea*
        Marlin fish
        Fishing for recreation
        Fishing as an industry
        The condition of our oceans
        The safety of our food supply from the oceans
        Overfishing
        Commercial fishing
        Careers in the fishing industry
        Cuba
        Caribbean waters
        Facts about baseball
        Biography of Joe DiMaggio
        Heroes of the past and present
        Living by a code
        Ocean life
        Boating
        Kinds of boats: their construction & uses

# NONFICTION ASSIGNMENT SHEET
## (To be completed after reading the required nonfiction article)

Name _____ Date _____

Title of Nonfiction Read _____

Written By _____ Publication Date _____

I. Factual Summary: Write a short summary of the piece you read.

II. Vocabulary
    1. With which vocabulary words in the piece did you encounter some degree of difficulty?

    2. How did you resolve your lack of understanding with these words?

III. Interpretation: What was the main point the author wanted you to get from reading his work?

IV. Criticism
    1. With which points of the piece did you agree or find easy to accept? Why?

    2. With which points of the piece did you disagree or find difficult to believe? Why?

V. Personal Response: What do you think about this piece? OR How does this piece influence your ideas?

# LESSON FOURTEEN

<u>Objectives</u>
1. To broaden students' knowledge of our world
2. To give students a little information about many topics related to the story
3. To give students the opportunity to practice public speaking
4. To evaluate students' retention of the nonfiction they read

<u>Activity</u>

Have each student stand in front of the class to give a short summary of the nonfiction he/she read relating to *The Old Man and the Sea*.

Note: The point is not to embarrass anyone; rather, to encourage students to be able to think on their feet, to be able to express themselves verbally even when they are in front of a group of people. This is a valuable skill for students to develop to help them prepare for adult life. As adults they will need to be able to stand up and express their opinions or give out a little information whether they are at a PTA meeting, a meeting at work, or in one of hundreds of other possible scenarios.

In addition, by hearing all the other reports, students will be exposed to all kinds of information instead of just their own reading.


# LESSON FIFTEEN

<u>Objectives</u>
1. To give students verbal, personal responses about their writing skills
2. To give students the opportunity to practice writing to inform
3. To give the teacher the opportunity to evaluate students' writing

<u>Activity #1</u>

Distribute Writing Assignment #2. Discuss the directions in detail and give students ample time to complete the assignment.

<u>Activity #2</u>

While students are working on Writing Assignment #2, call individual students to your desk or some other private area where you can have a writing conference based on Writing Assignment #1. An evaluation form is included with this unit to help guide your conferences if you wish to use it.

# WRITING ASSIGNMENT #2 - *The Old Man and The Sea*

## PROMPT
This writing assignment is to give you practice writing a composition to simply put forth information for your audience (readers).

The assignment is to write a composition about the nonfiction topics you reported about in the last class period.

## PREWRITING
Your research has already been done for you: use your Nonfiction Assignment Sheet and any other notes you may have taken.

## DRAFTING
Write an introductory paragraph in which you introduce the topic about which you read. Write one paragraph giving a short summary of the article. Write one paragraph telling the strengths of the article or book. Write one paragraph telling the weaknesses of the article or book. Write a concluding paragraph in which you tell the effect the article or book has had on you.

## PROMPT
When you finish the rough draft of your paper, ask a student who sits near you to read it. After reading your rough draft, he/she should tell you what he/she liked best about your work, which parts were difficult to understand, and ways in which your work could be improved. Reread your paper considering your critic's comments, and make the corrections you think are necessary.

## PROOFREADING
Do a final proofreading of your paper double-checking your grammar, spelling, organization, and the clarity of your ideas.

# WRITING EVALUATION FORM - *The Old Man and The Sea*

Name _____ Date _____

Writing Assignment #1 for the *Old Man and The Sea* unit   Grade _____

Circle One For Each Item:

Grammar:        correct        errors noted on paper

Spelling:       correct        errors noted on paper

Punctuation:    correct        errors noted on paper

Legibility:     excellent      good   fair   poor


Strengths:




Weaknesses:




Comments/Suggestions:

# LESSON SIXTEEN

Objective
   To review the main ideas presented in *The Old Man and The Sea*

Activity #1
   Choose one of the review games/activities included in the packet and spend your class period as outlined there. Some materials for these activities are located in the Unit Resources section of this unit.

Activity #2
   Remind students that the Unit Test will be in the next class meeting. Stress the review of April 27, 1994the Study Guides and their class notes as a last minute, brush-up review for homework.

# REVIEW GAMES/ACTIVITIES - *The Old Man and The Sea*

1. Ask the class to make up a unit test for *The Old Man and The Sea.* The test should have 4 sections: matching, true/false, short answer, and essay. Students may use 1/2 period to make the test and then swap papers and use the other 1/2 class period to take a test a classmate has devised. (open book) You may want to use the unit test included in this packet or take questions from the students' unit tests to formulate your own test.

2. Take 1/2 period for students to make up true and false questions (including the answers). Collect the papers and divide the class into two teams. Draw a big tic-tac-toe board on the chalk board. Make one team X and one team O. Ask questions to each side, giving each student one turn. If the question is answered correctly, that students' team's letter (X or O) is placed in the box. If the answer is incorrect, no mark is placed in the box. The object is to get three marks in a row like tic-tac-toe. You may want to keep track of the number of games won for each team.

3. Take 1/2 period for students to make up questions (true/false and short answer). Collect the questions. Divide the class into two teams. You'll alternate asking questions to individual members of teams A & B (like in a spelling bee). The question keeps going from A to B until it is correctly answered, then a new question is asked. A correct answer does not allow the team to get another question. Correct answers are +2 points; incorrect answers are -1 point.

4. Have students pair up and quiz each other from their study guides and class notes.

5. Give students a *The Old Man and The Sea* crossword puzzle to complete.

6. Divide your class into two teams. Use the *Old Man and The Sea* crossword words with their letters jumbled as a word list. Student 1 from Team A faces off against Student 1 from Team B. You write the first jumbled word on the board. The first student (1A or 1B) to unscramble the word wins the chance for his/her team to score points. If 1A wins the jumble, go to student 2A and give him/her a clue. He/she must give you the correct word which matches that clue. If he/she does, Team A scores a point, and you give student 3A a clue for which you expect another correct response. Continue giving Team A clues until some team member makes an incorrect response. An incorrect response sends the game back to the jumbled-word face off, this time with students 2A and 2B. Instead of repeating giving clues to the first few students of each team, continue with the student after the one who gave the last incorrect response on the team. For example, if Team B wins the jumbled-word face-off, and student 5B gave the last incorrect answer for Team B, you would start this round of clue questions with student 6B, and so on. The team with the most points wins!

# LESSON SEVENTEEN

Objective
   To test the students understanding of the main ideas and themes in *The Old Man and The Sea*

Activity #1
   Distribute the unit tests. Go over the instructions in detail and allow the students the entire class period to complete the exam.

NOTES ABOUT THE UNIT TESTS IN THIS UNIT:
   There are 5 different unit tests which follow.
   There are two short answer tests which are based primarily on facts from the novel.
   There is one advanced short answer unit test. It is based on the extra discussion questions and quotations. Use the matching key for short answer unit test 2 to check the matching section of the advanced short answer unit test. There is no key for the short answer questions and quotations. The answers will be based on the discussions you have had during class.
   There are two multiple choice unit tests. Following the two unit tests, you will find an answer sheet on which students should mark their answers. The same answer sheet should be used for both tests; however, students' answers will be different for each test. Following the students' answer sheet for the multiple choice tests you will find your answer keys.
   The short answer tests have a vocabulary section. You should choose 10 of the vocabulary words from this unit, read them orally and have the students write them down. Then, either have students write a definition or use the words in sentences.

   Use these words for the vocabulary section of the advanced short answer unit test:

| | | | |
|---|---|---|---|
| violated | placid | devise | mutilated |
| prolongs | endures | resolution | attained |
| congregated | humility | contempt | intolerable |

Activity #2
   Collect all test papers and assigned books prior to the end of the class period.

# LESSON EIGHTEEN

Objectives
    1. To give students the opportunity to express their personal opinions in writing
    2. To have students think about ways in which they are special--to evaluate their own talents and personal characteristics
    3. To give the teacher the opportunity to evaluate students' writing skills

Activity

    Distribute Writing Assignment #3. Discuss the directions in detail and give students ample time to complete the assignment.

    You may wish to give students this assignment to do when they finish their unit tests in Lesson Seventeen.

# WRITING ASSIGNMENT #3 - *The Old Man and the Sea*

## PROMPT
"There are many good fishermen and some great ones. But there is only you."

Your assignment is to write a composition entitled "But There Is Only One Me."

## PREWRITING
One way to start is to jot down on a piece of paper things that make you unique. What are your talents? What are your best characteristics? What are your worst characteristics? What things are in your experiences and how have they affected you?

## DRAFTING
Write an introductory paragraph in which you introduce the idea that you are a unique person. The paragraphs in the body of your composition should each discuss one way that you are unique, stating the fact and supporting the fact with examples. Write a concluding paragraph in which you bring your paper to a close and give your final remarks.

## PROMPT
When you finish the rough draft of your paper, ask a student who sits near you to read it. After reading your rough draft, he/she should tell you what he/she liked best about your work, which parts were difficult to understand, and ways in which your work could be improved. Reread your paper considering your critic's comments, and make the corrections you think are necessary.

## PROOFREADING
Do a final proofreading of your paper double-checking your grammar, spelling, organization, and the clarity of your ideas.

# UNIT TESTS

# SHORT ANSWER UNIT TEST 1 - *The Old Man and The Sea*

I. Matching/Identify

___ 1. Santiago         A. Kind of tuna
___ 2. DiMaggio       B. He received the head of the fish from Santiago
___ 3. Manolin         C. The old man
___ 4. Bonito          D. The old man's nickname
___ 5. Marlin          E. Baseball great
___ 6. Martin          F. The boy
___ 7. Pedrico        G. The big fish was this kind of fish
___ 8. El Campeon    H. Pub/restaurant owner

II. Short Answer

1. Why is there so much talk in the novel about baseball, specifically Joe DiMaggio?

2. What's Hemingway's point to having Santiago say, "I may not be as strong as I think . . . . But I know many tricks and I have resolution."

3. Give two examples of religious symbolism in the novel regarding Santiago and/or Manolin.

4. What problem did the old man have getting the fish home?

5. What of the fish was left when Santiago got back to port?

*Old Man* Short Answer Unit Test 1 Page 2

6. What are Santiago's feelings toward the marlin?

7. Describe Manolin's relationship with Santiago.

8. The old man apologizes to the fish. ("I am sorry that I went too far out. I ruined us both.") Why? What's the significance of this passage?

III. Composition
    You are Manolin. What would you say to convince your parents to let you go fishing with Santiago? Write in complete sentences and in paragraphs.

*Old Man* Short Answer Unit Test 1 Page 3

IV. Vocabulary

Listen to the vocabulary words and write them down. Go back later and write the correct definitions next to the words.

1.

2.

3.

4.

5.

6.

7.

8.

9.

10.

# SHORT ANSWER UNIT TEST 2 - *The Old Man and The Sea*

I. Matching

___ 1. Santiago          A. The old man's nickname
___ 2. DiMaggio        B. Pub/restaurant owner
___ 3. Manolin          C. The boy
___ 4. Bonito           D. The big fish was this kind of fish
___ 5. Marlin           E. The old man
___ 6. Martin           F. Baseball great
___ 7. Pedrico          G. Kind of tuna
___ 8. El Campeon    H. He received the head of the fish from Santiago

II. Short Answer

1. Why is the boy not fishing with the old man anymore? Does he want to?

2. "There are many good fishermen and some great ones. But there is only you." What does the boy mean?

3. "It is better to be lucky. But I would rather be exact. Then when luck comes, you are ready." Explain.

4. "If the others heard me talking out loud, they would think that I am crazy . . . But since I am not crazy, I do not care." What does that tell us about the old man's character?

*Old Man* Short Answer Unit Test 2 Page 2

5. "His choice had been to stay in the deep dark water far out beyond all snares and traps . . . My choice was to go there to find him beyond all people . . . in the world." Explain the importance of this passage.

6. Explain the significance of "Take a good rest, small bird . . . Then go in and take your chances like any man or bird or fish."

7. "But, thank God, they are not as intelligent as we who kill them, although they are more noble and more able." What's Hemingway saying?

8. Santiago feels he must "prove himself" to the fish and to the boy. "Now he was proving it again. Each time was a new time . . . ." What is the implication in broader terms; do we EVER stop having to prove ourselves (according to Hemingway)?

9. What are the old man's arguments with himself about whether or not killing the big fish is a sin? (What arguments does he make for and against it being a sin?)

10. Why does Manolin cry?

*Old Man* Short Answer Unit Test 2 Page 3

III. Composition
    What did the old man learn from his experience with the big fish? Write in paragraph form with complete sentences.

*Old Man* Short Answer Unit Test 2 Page 4

IV. Vocabulary

Listen to the vocabulary words and write them down. Go back later and write the correct definitions next to the words.

1.

2.

3.

4.

5.

6.

7.

8.

9.

10.

# KEY: SHORT ANSWER UNIT TESTS - *The Old Man and The Sea*

The short answer questions are taken directly from the study guides.
If you need to look up the answers, you will find them in the study guide section.

Answers to the composition questions will vary depending on your
class discussions and the level of your students.

For the vocabulary section of the test, choose ten of the
words from the vocabulary lists to read orally for your students.

The answers to the matching section of the test are below.

Answers to the matching section of the Advanced Short Answer Unit Test
are the same as for Short Answer Unit Test #1.

<u>Test #1</u>
1. C
2. E
3. F
4. A
5. G
6. H
7. B
8. D

<u>Test #2</u>
1. E
2. F
3. C
4. G
5. D
6. B
7. H
8. A

# ADVANCED SHORT ANSWER UNIT TEST - *The Old Man and The Sea*

I. Matching/Identify

___ 1. Santiago        A. The old man's nickname
___ 2. DiMaggio        B. Pub/restaurant owner
___ 3. Manolin         C. The boy
___ 4. Bonito          D. The big fish was this kind of fish
___ 5. Marlin          E. The old man
___ 6. Martin          F. Baseball great
___ 7. Pedrico         G. Kind of tuna
___ 8. El Campeon      H. He received the head of the fish from Santiago

II. Short Answer

1. Explain why the old man goes for the fish and stays with it until he brings the carcass to port even though he put himself at great risk to do so.

2. Compare Santiago to the marlin.

3. Compare and contrast Santiago and DiMaggio.

*Old Man* Advanced Unit Test Page 2

4. What function does the character of Manolin serve in the novel?

5. List three religious references in the story and explain why Hemingway chose this imagery.

6. Does Santiago undergo any type of change during the story? If so, what? If not, give possible reasons why he does not.

7. Explore the idea of nobility in the story.

8. "It is better to be lucky. But I would rather be exact. Then when luck comes, you are ready." Explain.

9. "If the others heard me talking out loud, they would think that I am crazy . . . But since I am not crazy, I do not care." What does that tell us about the old man's character?

10. "His choice had been to stay in the deep dark water far out beyond all snares and traps . . . My choice was to go there to find him beyond all people . . . in the world." Explain the importance of this passage.

*Old Man* Advanced Unit Test Page 3

III. Composition

There are many ideas one can get from reading *The Old Man and the Sea*. Write three paragraphs, one paragraph for each of three of the main ideas presented in the book.

IV. Vocabulary

Listen to the vocabulary words and write them down. Go back later and write a composition using all of the vocabulary words you are given. The composition must relate in some way to *The Old Man and the Sea*.

# MULTIPLE CHOICE UNIT TEST 1 - *The Old Man and The Sea*

I. Matching
- ___ 1. Santiago
- ___ 2. DiMaggio
- ___ 3. Manolin
- ___ 4. Bonito
- ___ 5. Marlin
- ___ 6. Martin
- ___ 7. Pedrico
- ___ 8. El Campeon

A. Kind of tuna
B. He received the head of the fish from Santiago
C. The old man
D. The old man's nickname
E. Baseball great
F. The boy
G. The big fish was this kind of fish
H. Pub/restaurant owner

II. Multiple Choice

1. Why is the boy not fishing with the old man anymore? Does he want to?
    a. Santiago is having a streak of bad luck. The boy's parents won't let him fish with Santiago even though he wants to.
    b. The boy has been offered a better paying job by one of the businessmen.
    c. The boy has had an accident while fishing. he is recuperating.
    d. Santiago and the boy had a fight because the boy was stealing fish. Santiago refused to take him fishing anymore.

2. Why is there so much talk about baseball, specifically Joe DiMaggio?
    a. Santiago identifies with DiMaggio, and sees that success is sometimes possible, no matter what the odds, if you want it enough.
    b. Baseball was the fishermen's only means of escape from the harshness of their existence.
    c. Santiago and the other men in the village had pooled their small savings and bet on DiMaggio's team to win. They listened to the games, hoping to become rich.
    d. DiMaggio's ancestors were from the village where Santiago lived. Santiago had known DiMaggio's grandfather when they were boys. The people of the village felt a personal kinship with him.

3. "There are many good fishermen and some great ones. But there is only you." What does the boy mean?
    a. It is a thinly disguised insult. Manolin has lost faith in Santiago.
    b. Manolin doesn't want to tell Santiago outright that he is really too old to be out fishing, so he tries to make subtle hints.
    c. Manolin means that Santiago is special. It could also mean that one has to use the talents one is given in life.
    d. He means that experience is the best teacher.

*Old Man* Multiple Choice Unit Test 1 Page 2

4. What is Hemingway's point to having the old man say, "I may not be as strong as I think . . . But I know many tricks and I have resolution?"
    a. He is telling the other fishermen that he doesn't want their help or their pity.
    b. Hemingway wants to make sure the readers fully understand the fisherman's character and motivations.
    c. Santiago is insulting the other fishermen, telling them that he is much wiser and more experienced. He is bitter because they don't respect him.
    d. Pure strength isn't the only important thing for a fisherman to have. If one is smart and persistent, he can accomplish great things without tremendous strength.

5. "It is better to be lucky. But I would rather be exact. Then when luck comes, you are ready." Explain.
    a. Good luck takes less work than exactness and yields better rewards.
    b. He knows that he has bad luck, so he is defending himself by saying that he prefers the other qualities.
    c. He made himself ready to take advantage of any lucky strike he might have by carefully preparing his fishing gear.
    d. Santiago believes that God will ultimately reward his patience and faith.

6. "If the other heard me talking out loud, they would think that I am crazy . . . But since I am not crazy, I do not care." What does that tell us about the old man's character?
    a. He knows himself and has the confidence not to care about what other people think.
    b. He is so out of touch that he doesn't realize he does things that seem crazy to others.
    c. He does not like the others so he deliberately does things to ostracize himself.
    d. He is really preoccupied with worrying about what the others think although he will not admit it.

7. "His choice had been to stay in the deep dark water far out beyond all snares and traps . . . My choice was to go there to find him beyond all people . . . in the world." Explain the importance of this passage.
    a. Santiago admits that the fish is wiser and more powerful than he is.
    b. Santiago is regretting that he ever went out after the fish. He realizes that he should have listened to the others.
    c. Santiago feels almost god-like in his capture and probable domination of the fish.
    d. Santiago has broken an unspoken law of nature and will pay a high price for hi sin.

*Old Man* Multiple Choice Unit Test 1 Page 3

8. Explain the significance of "Take a good rest, small bird . . . Then go in and take your chances like any man or bird or fish."
    a. If Santiago didn't catch the fish soon, he would kill and eat the bird.
    b. The bird could be safe with Santiago for a while, but would then have to fly on with his life, as all creatures must do.
    c. Santiago is getting deranged. He thinks the bird can understand him. This shows us his deteriorating mental and physical state.
    d. Santiago is really wishing he could take a rest, and that the bird could somehow help him.

9. "But, thank God, they are not as intelligent as we who kill them, although they are more noble and more able." What's Hemingway saying?
    a. If the fish had man's intelligence with its own nobility and ability, Santiago thinks men wouldn't be able to catch the fish.
    b. We shouldn't kill creatures that are not as smart as we are.
    c. God made the lower creatures less intelligent so we could catch them more easily.
    d. We are intelligent, but not intelligent enough to stop killing. This makes the lower animals more noble.

10. Santiago feels he must "prove himself" to the fish and to the boy. "Now he was proving it again. Each time was a new time . . . . " What is the implication in broader terms; do we EVER stop having to prove ourselves (according to Hemingway)?
    a. Once we have accomplished a task to our best ability we can stop proving ourselves.
    b. We can never do anything perfectly, so it is a waste of time to keep proving ourselves.
    c. If our past actions don't count for anything, and each new situation requires our best performance, then we must never stop proving ourselves.
    d. Since no one else's opinion really counts, we must each make the individual decision whether or not to prove ourselves to ourselves.

11. What are the old man's arguments with himself about killing the big fish?
    a. He argues about whether to share the profits from the fish or keep all of the money for himself.
    b. He argues about whether to use the fish as food for the villagers or to sell it to the fish brokers for profit.
    c. He argues about whether or not to abandon the fish's carcass in the water, since it is rapidly deteriorating anyway and since he has the knowledge of his victory.
    d. He argues about whether or not it is a sin to kill the fish.

*Old Man* Multiple Choice Unit Test 1 Page 4

12. A woman and her husband see the carcass of the magnificent fish and incorrectly identify it as a common shark of extraordinary size. What does this emphasize?
    a. Man's inability to recognize greatness in others
    b. The fall of the noble creature and the apparent insignificance of Santiago's great sin and battle
    c. Man's inability to celebrate the good fortune of another
    d. The impossibility of man's trying to conquer nature

*Old Man* Multiple Choice Unit Test 1 Page 5

IV. Vocabulary

___ 1. IMMUNE           A. A seat across a boat on which a rower may sit

___ 2. SCAVENGER        B. Marked by meekness or modesty in behavior

___ 3. INTOLERABLE      C. To carry on through despite hardships

___ 4. PLACID           D. To form, plan, or arrange in one's mind; design or contrive

___ 5. MALIGNANCY       E. Disfigured beyond repair

___ 6. BENEVOLENT       F. Producing a display of lustrous, rainbowlike colors

___ 7. MUTILATED        G. Units of length equal to six feet

___ 8. INEFFECTUAL      H. Characterized by or suggestive of doing good

___ 9. IRIDESCENT       I. Lowering the pride, dignity or self-respect

___ 10. ENDURES         J. Began; started

___ 11. DEVISE          K. Calm; quiet

___ 12. COMMENCED       L. A light, sharp-pointed sword lacking a cutting edge and used only for thrusting

___ 13. THWART          M. Something disposed to do evil; highly injurious

___ 14. ATTAINED        N. An animal that feeds on decaying matter

___ 15. HUMILIATING     O. Not affected by a given influence; unresponsive

___ 16. HUMILITY        P. Unbearable

___ 17. VIOLATED        Q. Insufficient to produce a desired effect

___ 18. FATHOMS         R. Gained as an objective; achieved

___ 19. RESOLUTION      S. Broke or disregarded

___ 20. RAPIER          T. Firm determination

# MULTIPLE CHOICE UNIT TEST 2 - *The Old Man and The Sea*

I. Matching
___ 1. Santiago            A. The old man's nickname
___ 2. DiMaggio            B. Pub/restaurant owner
___ 3. Manolin             C. The boy
___ 4. Bonito              D. The big fish was this kind of fish
___ 5. Marlin              E. The old man
___ 6. Martin              F. Baseball great
___ 7. Pedrico             G. Kind of tuna
___ 8. El Campeon          H. He received the head of the fish from Santiago

II. Multiple Choice
1. Why is the boy not fishing with the old man anymore? Does he want to?
    a. The boy has been offered a better paying job by one of the businessmen.
    b. Santiago is having a streak of bad luck. The boy's parents won't let him fish with Santiago even though he wants to.
    c. The boy has had an accident while fishing. he is recuperating.
    d. Santiago and the boy had a fight because the boy was stealing fish. Santiago refused to take him fishing anymore.

2. Why is there so much talk about baseball, specifically Joe DiMaggio?
    a. DiMaggio's ancestors were from the village where Santiago lived. Santiago had known DiMaggio's grandfather when they were boys. The people of the village felt a personal kinship with him.
    b. Baseball was the fishermen's only means of escape from the harshness of their existence.
    c. Santiago and the other men in the village had pooled their small savings and bet on DiMaggio's team to win. They listened to the games, hoping to become rich.
    d. Santiago identifies with DiMaggio, and sees that success is sometimes possible, no matter what the odds, if you want it enough.

3. "There are many good fishermen and some great ones. But there is only you." What does the boy mean?
    a. It is a thinly disguised insult. Manolin has lost faith in Santiago.
    b. Manolin means that Santiago is special. It could also mean that one has to use the talents one is given in life.
    c. Manolin doesn't want to tell Santiago outright that he is really too old to be out fishing, so he tries to make subtle hints.
    d. He means that experience is the best teacher.

*Old Man* Multiple Choice Unit Test 2 Page 2

4. What is Hemingway's point to having the old man say, "I may not be as strong as I think . . . But I know many tricks and I have resolution?"
    a. He is telling the other fishermen that he doesn't want their help or their pity.
    b. Hemingway wants to make sure the readers fully understand the fisherman's character and motivations.
    c. Pure strength isn't the only important thing for a fisherman to have. If one is smart and persistent, he can accomplish great things without tremendous strength.
    d. Santiago is insulting the other fishermen, telling them that he is much wiser and more experienced. He is bitter because they don't respect him.

5. "It is better to be lucky. But I would rather be exact. Then when luck comes, you are ready." Explain.
    a. He made himself ready to take advantage of any lucky strike he might have by carefully preparing his fishing gear.
    b. He knows that he has bad luck, so he is defending himself by saying that he prefers the other qualities.
    c. Good luck takes less work than exactness and yields better rewards.
    d. Santiago believes that God will ultimately reward his patience and faith.

6. "If the other heard me talking out loud, they would think that I am crazy . . . But since I am not crazy, I do not care." What does that tell us about the old man's character?
    a. He does not like the others so he deliberately does things to ostracize himself.
    b. He is so out of touch that he doesn't realize he does things that seem crazy to others.
    c. He knows himself and has the confidence not to care about what other people think.
    d. He is really preoccupied with worrying about what the others think although he will not admit it.

7. "His choice had been to stay in the deep dark water far out beyond all snares and traps . . . My choice was to go there to find him beyond all people . . . in the world." Explain the importance of this passage.
    a. Santiago admits that the fish is wiser and more powerful than he is.
    b. Santiago is regretting that he ever went out after the fish. He realizes that he should have listened to the others.
    c. Santiago has broken an unspoken law of nature and will pay a high price for his sin.
    d. Santiago feels almost god-like in his capture and probable domination of the fish.

*Old Man* Multiple Choice Unit Test 2 Page 3

8. Explain the significance of "Take a good rest, small bird . . . Then go in and take your chances like any man or bird or fish."
    a. If Santiago didn't catch the fish soon, he would kill and eat the bird.
    b. Santiago is really wishing he could take a rest, and that the bird could somehow help him.
    c. Santiago is getting deranged. He thinks the bird can understand him. This shows us his deteriorating mental and physical state.
    d. The bird could be safe with Santiago for a while, but would then have to fly on with his life, as all creatures must do.

9. "But, thank God, they are not as intelligent as we who kill them, although they are more noble and more able." What's Hemingway saying?
    a. We shouldn't kill creatures that are not as smart as we are.
    b. If the fish had man's intelligence with its own nobility and ability, Santiago thinks men wouldn't be able to catch the fish.
    c. God made the lower creatures less intelligent so we could catch them more easily.
    d. We are intelligent, but not intelligent enough to stop killing. This makes the lower animals more noble.

10. Santiago feels he must "prove himself" to the fish and to the boy. "Now he was proving it again. Each time was a new time . . . . " What is the implication in broader terms; do we EVER stop having to prove ourselves (according to Hemingway)?
    a. If our past actions don't count for anything, and each new situation requires our best performance, then we must never stop proving ourselves.
    b. Since no one else's opinion really counts, we must each make the individual decision whether or not to prove ourselves to ourselves.
    c. Once we have accomplished a task to our best ability we can stop proving ourselves.
    d. We can never do anything perfectly, so it is a waste of time to keep proving ourselves.

11. What are the old man's arguments with himself about killing the big fish?
    a. He argues about whether or not it is a sin to kill the fish.
    b. He argues about whether to use the fish as food for the villagers or to sell it to the fish brokers for profit.
    c. He argues about whether or not to abandon the fish's carcass in the water, since it is rapidly deteriorating anyway and since he has the knowledge of his victory.
    d. He argues about whether to share the profits from the fish or keep all of the money for himself.

*Old Man* Multiple Choice Unit Test 2 Page 4

12. A woman and her husband see the carcass of the magnificent fish and incorrectly identify it as a common shark of extraordinary size. What does this emphasize?
    a. Man's inability to recognize greatness in others
    b. Man's inability to celebrate the good fortune of another
    c. The fall of the noble creature and the apparent insignificance of Santiago's great sin and battle
    d. The impossibility of man's trying to conquer nature

*Old Man* Multiple Choice Unit Test 2 Page 5

IV. Vocabulary

___ 1. BENEVOLENT          A. Calm; quiet

___ 2. ENDURES             B. An animal that feeds on decaying matter

___ 3. PLACID              C. Broke or disregarded

___ 4. SCAVENGER           D. Began; started

___ 5. RESOLUTION          E. Rolled up and secured to something

___ 6. SUSTENANCE          F. Disfigured beyond repair

___ 7. DEVISE              G. Scorn; disparaging or haughty disdain

___ 8. IRIDESCENT          H. Firm determination

___ 9. MALIGNANCY          I. A light, sharp-pointed sword lacking a cutting edge and used only for thrusting

___ 10. CONTEMPT           J. Characterized by or suggestive of doing good

___ 11. INEFFECTUAL        K. Producing a display of lustrous, rainbowlike colors

___ 12. HUMILIATING        L. To carry on through despite hardships

___ 13. RAPIER             M. Lowering the pride, dignity or self-respect

___ 14. IMMUNE             N. To form, plan, or arrange in one's mind; design or contrive

___ 15. THWART             O. Something, esp. food, that sustains life or health

___ 16. MUTILATE           P. A seat across a boat on which a rower may sit

___ 17. FURLED             Q. Something disposed to do evil; highly injurious

___ 18. COMMENCED          R. Insufficient to produce a desired effect

___ 19. ATTAINED           S. Gained as an objective; achieved

___ 20. VIOLATED           T. Not affected by a given influence; unresponsive

## ANSWER SHEET - *The Old Man and The Sea*
## Multiple Choice Unit Tests

I. Matching
1. ___
2. ___
3. ___
4. ___
5. ___
6. ___
7. ___
8. ___

II. Multiple Choice
1. ___
2. ___
3. ___
4. ___
5. ___
6. ___
7. ___
8. ___
9. ___
10. ___
11. ___
12. ___

IV. Vocabulary
1. ___
2. ___
3. ___
4. ___
5. ___
6. ___
7. ___
8. ___
9. ___
10. ___
11. ___
12. ___
13. ___
14. ___
15. ___
16. ___
17. ___
18. ___
19. ___
20. ___

# ANSWER KEY MULTIPLE CHOICE UNIT TESTS – *The Old Man and The Sea*

Answers to Unit Test 1 are in the left column. Answers to Unit Test 2 are in the right column.

| I. Matching | II. Multiple Choice | IV. Vocabulary |
|---|---|---|
| 1. C   E | 1. A   B | 1. O   J |
| 2. E   F | 2. A   D | 2. N   L |
| 3. F   C | 3. C   B | 3. P   A |
| 4. A   G | 4. D   C | 4. K   B |
| 5. G   D | 5. C   A | 5. M   H |
| 6. H   B | 6. A   C | 6. H   O |
| 7. B   H | 7. D   C | 7. E   N |
| 8. D   A | 8. B   D | 8. Q   K |
|  | 9. A   B | 9. F   Q |
|  | 10. C   A | 10. C   G |
|  | 11. D   A | 11. D   R |
|  | 12. B   C | 12. J   M |
|  |  | 13. A   I |
|  |  | 14. R   T |
|  |  | 15. I   P |
|  |  | 16. B   F |
|  |  | 17. S   E |
|  |  | 18. G   D |
|  |  | 19. T   S |
|  |  | 20. L   C |

# UNIT RESOURCE MATERIALS

# BULLETIN BOARD IDEAS - *The Old Man and The Sea*

1. Save one corner of the board for the best of students' *The Old Man and The Sea* writing assignments.

2. Title the board "WE ARE BROTHERS" in cut-out letters. Put up a collage of nature scenes and animals from magazines, the library or other sources. (You may ask students to find pictures as an assignment and have each one put up his picture on the bulletin board).

3. Take one of the word search puzzles from the extra activities packet and with a marker copy it over in a large size on the bulletin board. Write the clue words to find to one side. Invite students prior to and after class to find the words and circle them on the bulletin board.

4. Do a bulletin board about careers in the fishing industry

5. Do a bulletin board with information about how to create goals for oneself and how to maintain the resolution to achieve those goals.

6. Write several of the most significant quotations from the book onto the board on brightly colored paper.

7. Have students bring in things (pictures, drawings, anything that can be attached to your bulletin board) which represent their heroes. See Lesson Three.

8. Make a bulletin board listing the vocabulary words for this unit. As you complete sections of the novel and discuss the vocabulary for each section, write the definitions on the bulletin board. (If your board is one students face frequently, it will help them learn the words.)

9. Make a bulletin board about Hemingway. Write a brief biography of Hemingway in the center of the board and post book covers (either real ones or ones made of construction paper) of his most noteworthy books around the biography.

# EXTRA ACTIVITIES

One of the difficulties in teaching a novel is that all students don't read at the same speed. One student who likes to read may take the book home and finish it in a day or two. Sometimes a few students finish the in-class assignments early. The problem, then, is finding suitable extra activities for students.

The best thing I've found is to keep a little library in the classroom. For this unit on *The Old Man and The Sea,* you might check out from the school library other novels and stories by Hemingway. A biography or articles about the author would be interesting for some students. You can include other related books and articles about careers in journalism, histories about the wars Hemingway was involved in, information and articles about hunting, fishing, athletics, bullfights, etc., or articles of criticism about his works.

Other things you may keep on hand are puzzles. We have made some relating directly to *The Old Man and The Sea* for you. Feel free to duplicate them.

Some students may like to draw. You might devise a contest or allow some extra-credit grade for students who draw characters or scenes from *The Old Man and The Sea.* Note, too, that if the students do not want to keep their drawings you may pick up some extra bulletin board materials this way. If you have a contest and you supply the prize (a CD or something like that perhaps), you could, possibly, make the drawing itself a non-refundable entry fee.

The pages which follow contain games, puzzles and worksheets. The keys, when appropriate, immediately follow the puzzle or worksheet. There are two main groups of activities: one group for the unit; that is, generally relating to the *Old Man and The Sea* text, and another group of activities related strictly to the *Old Man and The Sea* vocabulary.

Directions for these games, puzzles and worksheets are self-explanatory. The object here is to provide you with extra materials you may use in any way you choose.

# MORE ACTIVITIES - *The Old Man and The Sea*

1. Have students design a book cover (front and back and inside flaps) for *The Old Man and The Sea.*

2. Have students design a bulletin board (ready to be put up; not just sketched) for *The Old Man and The Sea.*

3. Have a guest speaker discuss current commercial fishing techniques and problems.

4. Use some of the related topics (noted earlier for an in-class library) as topics for research, reports or written papers, or as topics for guest speakers.

5. Research what careers are currently available in the commercial fishing industry.

6. Give students the writing assignment of describing an event using Hemingway's writing style.

7. Have students write parodies of *The Old Man and The Sea.*

8. Display model fishing boats to show the different sizes through the years.

9. Spend a day showing/discussing survival skills. Perhaps have a film or guest speaker one day and a follow-up discussion the next day.

10. Have students (or groups of students) make tape recordings of their parodies.

11. If you live in an area where fishing is popular, have a fishing "show and tell" so students can practice speaking in front of a group.

12. Write a poem about the old man's experience with the fish.

13. Pretend you are Manolin. Write a letter for Santiago to read offshore.

14. Research people who have risked their lives to battle nature: explorers, adventurers, scientists, dare-devils, athletes, etc.

# WORD SEARCH - *The Old Man and The Sea*

All words in this list are associated with *The Old Man and The Sea*. The words are placed backwards, forward, diagonally, up and down. The included words are listed below the word searches.

```
V H L M T G Q O P Y C D N R D D V R J P Y K V S
J B N X C C G J P W F O Y T H I D B V W Q W D K
K L K G V A J L D V E F F A Y T M S G J R G T Q
B D F C I M G N Z P L W R W C J R A T Q K C T J
N S Q T L L Z J M B K P R S D M H I G R F J S N
V H N U T V I A N F O T K I A R Q S C G Q L E Q
D A C H C Y C O V O F V C S C K D F E K I W M G
S K I F F L Y I N G B A T E Y E O A L A S O N V
P T V S E P U I L S R E G I F T X S S P A I F N
B E E G F K H B N C W M J E A C V A A R T C I W
B H D N W P D J A S B G A Z W B R P C R R L T V
R O J R L F C S R E H T O R B R E A A T O W E D
C C N O I S S U H G P A K B L R E M M N T L S J
P H D I B C N D B A P P R D S I K S A P K Y P L
R F B K T B O M B A C H Q K F Y N M T W S K D N
R T B X B O J L D D H K B M S J B S H L M C J K
V D X Z R K V Q F S T L V G X S C V F S I K S H
D C H G R M S S M J L C W G C P H D H R B N V Y
S J X R B F C M X Q N D K G R C H H C K Q T G C
F W N F Z V H Q K K J L B K B M V T C Q Q Y Q
```

| | | | |
|---|---|---|---|
| BAIT | DOLPHIN | MARLIN | SANTIAGO |
| BAT | ELCAMPEON | MARTIN | SEA |
| BONITO | EXACT | MAST | SHACK |
| BROTHERS | EYE | NETS | SHARKS |
| CARCASS | FLYING | NEWSPAPER | SKIFF |
| CLUB | GAFF | OAR | TOWED |
| CRAMPS | HARPOON | PEDRICO | TRICKS |
| CUBA | LIONS | RICE | WET |
| DEFEAT | LUCK | SAILS | WRESTLING |
| DIMAGGIO | MANOLIN | SALAO | |

# CROSSWORD - *The Old Man and The Sea*

# CROSSWORD CLUES - *Old Man and the Sea*

### ACROSS

1. Santiago's muscular problem with his hands
2. Subject of the old man's dreams
6. It holds a sail.
9. El Campeon; the old man
12. Pub/restaurant owner
14. Loss
16. S. ate ---- fish from the bigger fish's stomach.
17. Opposite of on
18. Fish lure
19. Santiago had a streak of bad ----
22. They can power a boat with the wind.
26. S. got his nickname from arm ---- in his youth.
28. Sharp instrument that finally killed the big fish
30. Baseball club
31. S. does this to his hands to keep them useful
33. Santiago's hands were ---
35. Mister; man's respectful name
36. Second kind of fish Santiago ate
37. Positive attitude; able to do
38. Distress signal
39. Baseball great
41. The fish are our -----.
43. Fish use these to get oxygen from water
45. S. cut ---- the little fish to clean them
46. String with a hook at the end
47. Tired
48. Opposite of out
49. S. got a cut below his --- when the fish pulled him over.
50. Kind of fish the old man caught
51. Necessities

### DOWN

1. Santiago's home country
3. S. tied his knife to one to make a weapon.
4. Santiago's kind of boat
5. Edible nourishment
7. The worst kind of bad luck
8. Yellow ---; a friendly, wishful joke
9. Ocean
10. Tied rope-like things that catch fish
11. Large hook with which one pulls in a lined fish
12. The boy
13. S. got a cut below his --- when the fish pulled him over.
15. It is better to be lucky. But I would rather be ---
20. Santiago hit the sharks with one.
21. He received the head of the fish from Santiago
22. Small house, usually run-down
23. They attacked and ate the big fish.
24. I know many --- and I have resolution.
25. What the big fish did to Santiago's boat
26. The fish's splash got Santiago all ---.
27. Daily news publication
29. Leftover bones
32. Kind of tuna
34. The old man
39. The small fish were this meal for Santiago
40. The old man was ---; by himself
42. Exhausted
43. When the meat of the fish was ---, the sharks went away
44. Bang against; hit with a hard blow
47. Have a victory

# CROSSWORD - *The Old Man and The Sea*

# MATCHING QUIZ/WORKSHEET 1 - *The Old Man and The Sea*

___ 1. CRAMPS     A. Santiago hit the sharks with one.

___ 2. EYE     B. Sharp instrument that finally killed the big fish

___ 3. HARPOON     C. Santiago's muscular problem with his hands

___ 4. SHARKS     D. They attacked and ate the big fish.

___ 5. PEDRICO     E. They can power a boat with the wind.

___ 6. NETS     F. He received the head of the fish from Santiago

___ 7. BONITO     G. Kind of tuna

___ 8. EXACT     H. S. got a cut below his --- when the fish pulled him over.

___ 9. NEWSPAPER     I. The fish are our -----.

___ 10. MANOLIN     J. The boy

___ 11. WRESTLING     K. It is better to be lucky. But I would rather be ---

___ 12. MARTIN     L. Tied rope-like things that catch fish

___ 13. SEA     M. It holds a sail.

___ 14. SAILS     N. Santiago had a streak of bad ----

___ 15. LUCK     O. The fish's splash got Santiago all ---.

___ 16. CLUB     P. Pub/restaurant owner

___ 17. CUBA     Q. Ocean

___ 18. BROTHERS     R. Daily news publication

___ 19. WET     S. Santiago's home country

___ 20. MAST     T. S. got his nickname from arm ---- in his youth.

# MATCHING QUIZ/WORKSHEET 2 - *The Old Man and The Sea*

___ 1. CARCASS         A. Sharp instrument that finally killed the big fish

___ 2. BAT             B. Ocean

___ 3. NEWSPAPER       C. Leftover bones

___ 4. DOLPHIN         D. The boy

___ 5. SAILS           E. They can power a boat with the wind.

___ 6. SEA             F. What the big fish did to Santiago's boat

___ 7. MANOLIN         G. Loss

___ 8. DEFEAT          H. Fish lure

___ 9. EXACT           I. Santiago had a streak of bad ----

___ 10. LUCK           J. The old man

___ 11. MARTIN         K. Large hook with which one pulls in a lined fish

___ 12. RICE           L. It is better to be lucky. But I would rather be ---

___ 13. BONITO         M. Second kind of fish Santiago ate

___ 14. GAFF           N. Daily news publication

___ 15. TOWED          O. S. got his nickname from arm ---- in his youth.

___ 16. FLYING         P. S. ate ---- fish from the bigger fish's stomach.

___ 17. WRESTLING      Q. Yellow ---; a friendly, wishful joke

___ 18. HARPOON        R. Kind of tuna

___ 19. BAIT           S. Baseball club

___ 20. ELCAMPEON      T. Pub/restaurant owner

# KEY: MATCHING QUIZ/WORKSHEETS - *The Old Man and The Sea*

| Worksheet 1 | Worksheet 2 |
| --- | --- |
| 1. C | 1. C |
| 2. H | 2. S |
| 3. B | 3. N |
| 4. D | 4. M |
| 5. F | 5. E |
| 6. L | 6. B |
| 7. G | 7. D |
| 8. K | 8. G |
| 9. R | 9. L |
| 10. J | 10. I |
| 11. T | 11. T |
| 12. P | 12. Q |
| 13. Q | 13. R |
| 14. E | 14. K |
| 15. N | 15. F |
| 16. A | 16. P |
| 17. S | 17. O |
| 18. I | 18. A |
| 19. O | 19. H |
| 20. M | 20. J |

# JUGGLE LETTER REVIEW GAME CLUE SHEET - *The Old Man and The Sea*

| SCRAMBLED | WORD | CLUE |
|---|---|---|
| GNIYFL | FLYING | Santiago ate --- fish from the bigger fish's stomach |
| ANSPEEWRP | NEWSPAPER | Daily news publication |
| IKSRCT | TRICKS | I know many --- and I have resolution |
| ISLSA | SAILS | They help power a boat using wind. |
| FFAG | GAFF | Large hook used to bring in a lined fish |
| ERIC | RICE | Yellow ---; a friendly, wishful joke between friends |
| IDCORPE | PEDRICO | He received the head of the fish from Santiago |
| TAEDEF | DEFEAT | Loss |
| OSLIN | LIONS | Subject of the old man's dreams from Africa |
| AMNRLI | MARLIN | Kind of fish the old man caught |
| OENPLMCEA | ELCAMPEON | The old man's nickname |
| GIAOGDIM | DIMAGGIO | Baseball great |
| GSNERIWLT | WRESTLING | Santiago got his nickname from arm --- in his youth. |
| WDETO | TOWED | What the big fish did to Santiago's boat |
| ULKC | LUCK | Santiago had a streak of bad ---. |
| AGANSOIT | SANTIAGO | El Campeon; the old man |
| EAS | SEA | *The Old Man and the ---* |
| ARSACSC | CARCASS | Leftover bones |
| OPHLIND | DOLPHIN | Second kind of fish Santiago ate |
| ONBTOI | BONITO | Kind of tuna |
| ROA | OAR | Santiago tied his knife to one to make a weapon. |
| ATB | BAT | Baseball stick |
| FIFSK | SKIFF | Santiago's kind of boat |
| CETXA | EXACT | It is better to be lucky. But I would rather be -- |
| YEE | EYE | Santiago got a cut below his --- |
| PONROAH | HARPOON | Sharp instrument that finally killed the big fish |
| ETW | WET | The fish's splash got Santiago all --- |
| APMSRC | CRAMPS | Santiago's muscular problem with his hands |
| TSMA | MAST | It holds a sail. |
| ALOSA | SALAO | The worst kind of bad luck |
| OMINANL | MANOLIN | The boy |
| UCAB | CUBA | Santiago's home country |
| KACHS | SHACK | Small house, usually run-down |
| ANIMTR | MARTIN | Pub/restaurant owner |
| ATBI | BAIT | Fish lure |
| RKSHSA | SHARKS | They attacked and ate the big fish |
| ESNT | NETS | Tied rope-like things that catch lots of fish |

# VOCABULARY RESOURCE MATERIALS

# VOCABULARY WORD SEARCH - *The Old Man and The Sea*

All words in this list are associated with *The Old Man and The Sea* with an emphasis on the vocabulary words chosen for study in the text. The words are placed backwards, forward, diagonally, up and down. The included words are listed below.

```
I N E F F E C T U A L H C O N G R E G A T E D V
T W L X B Q P P M T M X U O N B T Q Z H T E K M
Y W S F V R V B F Q D V I M F D V Y R X T P T X
S S R K F M D N H R B T V Y I D F H B A L L T G
W Q M Y R S G L C N U M N H W L Z J L W G C S M
G S P G D S U J Q L J C M D X K I O V L K Q T F
X N R R C V B S O G S X E U S L I A B L C S X C
B P X C O M Q S T S N C P C T V R H T S Q Y Q W
T R X P K L E J K E N X A G Y I J A L I C J P H
X C S I T R O B N E N D L V B T L N P N N S L W
R J C Y N H W N M C B A N T E D B A A I G G M Y
J T J T W T Q M G G N Q N K I N Q N T Q E T L H
P H O S P H O R E S C E N C E D G T D E L R U F
G T R J F C P L M H L X A P E I P E S R D M S T
W B P H I Y S O E O L L C N L M H I R J I E R C
J X N T W M H F V R P D I A E D V C M L R P M B
T H W A R T M E J D A A M T G E B N I U M W P R
K V D V A P N U B H T B N N D F P T D J M X B F
L Q X F M E G H N T S O L C L S Y N M Z P H N L
R N Z W B C Y B A E C T N E C S E D I R I H B J
```

| | | | |
|---|---|---|---|
| ATTAINED | FATHOMS | IRIDESCENT | RESOLUTION |
| BENEVOLENT | FURLED | MALIGNANCY | SCAVENGER |
| COMMENCED | HUMILIATING | MUTILATED | SUSTENANCE |
| CONGREGATED | HUMILITY | PHOSPHORESCENCE | THWART |
| CONTEMPT | IMMUNE | PLACID | VIOLATED |
| DEVISE | INEFFECTUAL | PROLONGS | |
| ENDURES | INTOLERABLE | RAPIER | |

# VOCABULARY CROSSWORD - *The Old Man and The Sea*

# VOCABULARY CROSSWORD CLUES - *Old Man and the Sea*

ACROSS
1. Yellow ---; a friendly, wishful joke
3. Scorn; disparaging or haughty disdain
7. Loss
10. Fish lure
11. Not affected by a given influence; unresponsive
13. The fish's splash got Santiago all ---.
16. Insufficient to produce a desired effect
18. It holds the fishing line on the pole; ---- in the fish
19. The sun rises from this direction
20. Had a debt to
22. Rest against something
24. A light, sharp-pointed sword lacking a cutting edge and used only for thrusting
25. Gained as an objective; achieved
27. Subject of the old man's dreams
28. I know many --- and I have resolution.
33. S. tied his knife to one to make a weapon.
34. Characterized by or suggestive of doing good
37. An animal that feeds on decaying matter
38. Santiago had a streak of bad ----
41. Santiago's muscular problem with his hands
43. Began; started
46. To lengthen in duration; protract
49. The final one
50. Color of night
51. Something, esp. food, that sustains life or health
52. Pub/restaurant owner
53. Questioned

DOWN
2. Producing a display of lustrous, rainbow-like colors
3. Gathered; assembled
4. A seat across a boat on which a rower may sit
5. Disfigured beyond repair
6. Large hook with which one pulls in a fish one has caught
8. Rolled up and secured to something
9. What the big fish did to Santiago's boat
12. Something disposed to do evil; highly injurious
14. Firm determination
15. Lowering the pride, dignity or self-respect
17. To carry on through despite hardships
21. Small house, usually run-down
23. Broke or disregarded
26. S. got a cut below his --- when the fish pulled him over.
29. Santiago's home country
30. They attacked and ate the big fish.
31. Tied rope-like things that catch fish
32. Calm; quiet
34. Baseball club
35. Units of length equal to six feet
36. Ocean
39. Leftover bones
40. Worked
41. Santiago hit the sharks with one.
42. Choose
44. It holds a sail.
45. It is better to be lucky. But I would rather be ---
47. Singular
48. Grasp

## VOCABULARY CROSSWORD ANSWER KEY - *The Old Man and The Sea*

## VOCABULARY WORKSHEET 1 - *The Old Man and The Sea*

___ 1. MALIGNANCY          A. Disfigured beyond repair

___ 2. IMMUNE               B. Broke or disregarded

___ 3. INTOLERABLE          C. To form, plan, or arrange in one's mind; design or contrive

___ 4. PHOSPHORESCENCE      D. A light, sharp-pointed sword lacking a cutting edge and used only for thrusting

___ 5. ATTAINED             E. Characterized by or suggestive of doing good

___ 6. RAPIER               F. Marked by meekness or modesty in behavior

___ 7. BENEVOLENT           G. Gained as an objective; achieved

___ 8. INEFFECTUAL          H. Not affected by a given influence; unresponsive

___ 9. IRIDESCENT           I. A seat across a boat on which a rower may sit

___ 10. PLACID              J. Emission of light without burning

___ 11. DEVISE              K. Units of length equal to six feet

___ 12. HUMILIATING         L. Calm; quiet

___ 13. HUMILITY            M. Unbearable

___ 14. CONTEMPT            N. Something disposed to do evil; highly injurious

___ 15. THWART              O. Lowering the pride, dignity or self-respect

___ 16. PROLONGS            P. Insufficient to produce a desired effect

___ 17. VIOLATED            Q. Producing a display of lustrous, rainbowlike colors

___ 18. MUTILATED           R. Scorn; disparaging or haughty disdain

___ 19. FURLED              S. To lengthen in duration; protract

___ 20. FATHOMS             T. Rolled up and secured to something

# VOCABULARY WORKSHEET 2 - *The Old Man and The Sea*

___ 1. CONGREGATED         A. To lengthen in duration; protract

___ 2. PROLONGS             B. Gathered; assembled

___ 3. INTOLERABLE          C. Marked by meekness or modesty in behavior

___ 4. CONTEMPT             D. Scorn; disparaging or haughty disdain

___ 5. ENDURES              E. A light, sharp-pointed sword lacking a cutting edge and used only for thrusting

___ 6. RESOLUTION           F. Broke or disregarded

___ 7. MUTILATED            G. Insufficient to produce a desired effect

___ 8. INEFFECTUAL          H. Unbearable

___ 9. PLACID               I. Producing a display of lustrous, rainbowlike colors

___ 10. FURLED              J. Gained as an objective; achieved

___ 11. ATTAINED            K. Rolled up and secured to something

___ 12. VIOLATED            L. Calm; quiet

___ 13. COMMENCED           M. Units of length equal to six feet

___ 14. HUMILITY            N. An animal that feeds on decaying matter

___ 15. RAPIER              O. Emission of light without burning

___ 16. BENEVOLENT          P. Disfigured beyond repair

___ 17. PHOSPHORESCENCE     Q. Characterized by or suggestive of doing good

___ 18. FATHOMS             R. Firm determination

___ 19. SCAVENGER           S. To carry on through despite hardships

___ 20. IRIDESCENT          T. Began; started

# KEY: VOCABULARY WORKSHEETS - *The Old Man and The Sea*

| Worksheet 1 | Worksheet 2 |
|---|---|
| 1. N | 1. B |
| 2. H | 2. A |
| 3. M | 3. H |
| 4. J | 4. D |
| 5. G | 5. S |
| 6. D | 6. R |
| 7. E | 7. P |
| 8. P | 8. G |
| 9. Q | 9. L |
| 10. L | 10. K |
| 11. C | 11. J |
| 12. O | 12. F |
| 13. F | 13. T |
| 14. R | 14. C |
| 15. I | 15. E |
| 16. S | 16. Q |
| 17. B | 17. O |
| 18. A | 18. M |
| 19. T | 19. N |
| 20. K | 20. I |

# VOCABULARY JUGGLE LETTER REVIEW GAME CLUES - *The Old Man and The Sea*

| SCRAMBLED | WORD | CLUE |
|---|---|---|
| DOITVALE | VIOLATED | Broke or disregarded |
| PEONSEEHPRHCOCS | PHOSPHORESCENCE | Emission of light without burning |
| UMTEADILT | MUTILATED | Disfigured beyond repair |
| IACDLP | PLACID | Calm; quiet |
| LNENEETBOV | BENEVOLENT | Characterized by or suggestive of doing good |
| AIUNITLGHMI | HUMILIATING | Lowering the pride, dignity or self-respect |
| EVSDEI | DEVISE | To form, plan or arrange in one's mind; design or contrive |
| SUEEDNR | ENDURES | Carries on through despite hardships |
| TREELANLIBO | INTOLERABLE | Unbearable |
| NLGOROSP | PROLONGS | Lengthens in duration; protracts |
| ELDFUR | FURLED | Rolled up and secured to something |
| ARREIP | RAPIER | A light, sharp-pointed sword with no cutting edge |
| ILUTYMHI | HUMILITY | Marked by meekness or modesty in behavior |
| ARTWHT | THWART | A boat seat |
| EDCMMCONE | COMMENCED | Began; started |
| CEGRNAEVS | SCAVENGER | An animal that feeds on decaying matter |
| EGACDROENTG | CONGREGATED | Gathered; assembled |
| NUOITLOSER | RESOLUTION | Firm determination |
| EFAILEUCNTF | INEFFECTUAL | Insufficient to produce a desired effect |
| AEENTCSNUS | SUSTENANCE | Something that sustains life or health |
| TNATDEAI | ATTAINED | Gained as an objective; achieved |
| TEPTOCMN | CONTEMPT | Scorn; haughty disdain |
| OFHMSAT | FATHOMS | Units of length equal to six feet |
| IEENDCSRTI | IRIDESCENT | Producing lustrous, rainbow-like colors |

www.ingramcontent.com/pod-product-compliance
Lightning Source LLC
Chambersburg PA
CBHW051418070526
44584CB00023B/3486